The politics of town planning

POLITICS TODAY

General Editors: *Bernard Crick, Patrick Seyd*

THE POLITICS OF NATIONALISM AND DEVOLUTION
  H. M. Drucker and Gordon Brown
THE POLITICS OF POVERTY   *Susanne MacGregor*
THE POLITICS OF TOWN PLANNING   *Gordon Cherry*
THE POLITICS OF LOCAL AND REGIONAL GOVERNMENT
  Alan Alexander

Forthcoming:

THE POLITICS OF WOMEN'S RIGHTS   *April Carter*
THE POLITICS OF THE INNER CITIES   *Geoffrey Green*
THE POLITICS OF SEXUAL MORALITY   *Cate Haste*
THE POLITICS OF HEALTH CARE   *Rudolf Klein*
THE POLITICS OF PENAL REFORM   *Mick Ryan*
THE POLITICS OF ENERGY   *Roger Williams*
THE POLITICS OF TRANSPORT   *Enid Wistrich*
THE POLITICS OF LAW AND ORDER   *Michael Zander*

POLITICAL ISSUES IN MODERN BRITAIN
Published by Fontana

THE POLITICS OF THE JUDICIARY   *J. A. G. Griffith*
THE POLITICS OF EDUCATIONAL CHANGE   *Maurice Kogan*
THE POLITICS OF ECONOMIC PLANNING   *Alan Budd*
THE POLITICS OF THE MEDIA   *John Whale*
THE POLITICS OF INDUSTRIAL RELATIONS   *Colin Crouch*

THE POLITICS OF TOWN PLANNING

Gordon E. Cherry

LONGMAN
London and New York

LONGMAN GROUP LIMITED
Longman House
Burnt Mill, Harlow, Essex, UK

*Published in the United States of America
by Longman Inc., New York*

First published 1982

BRITISH LIBRARY CATALOGUING IN PUBLICATION DATA

Cherry, Gordon E.
  The politics of town planning. –
  (Politics today)
  1. Cities and towns – Planning –
  Great Britain 2. Regional
  planning – Great Britain
  I. Title   II. Series
  711'.0941   HT395.G7
  ISBN 0-582-29540-8

LIBRARY OF CATALOGING IN PUBLICATION DATA

Cherry, Gordon Emanuel.
  The politics of town planning.

  (Politics today)
  Bibliography: p.
  Includes index.
  1.   City planning – Great Britain.   I. Title.
  II.   Series.
  HT169.G7C4596   307.7'6'0941   81-20772
  ISBN 0–582–29540–8   AACR2

Printed in Singapore by
The Print House (Pte) Ltd.

CONTENTS

EDITORS' PREFACE

There is a demand among the general public as well as from students for books that deal with the main issues of modern British politics in such a way that the reader can gain a reliable account of how an issue arose, of its institutional context and then, but only then, to have argument about what should be done.

Behind what have become political issues, there are fundamental problems. Many books identify these problems theoretically, but too often ignore the empirical context, and others are so polemical and doctrinaire, that their conclusions, however just, are distrusted by shrewd readers. We believe in casting out neither facts nor values, but in relating them closely but distinctly. The test of a good book on political issues should be that a reader will feel that he has a full and reliable account of how the issue arose and what institutions and groups affect and are affected by it, irrespective of what the author thinks should be done. But authors cannot just describe, inevitably they prescribe; so let it be done openly and clearly. Politics is too important for neutrality, but therefore demanding of objectivity. So we ask the authors in this series to organise the books into three parts: the recent history of the matter, the institutional setting, and argument about the future.

We believe that relevant books are wanted, neither wholly committed books nor those that pretend to scientific objectivity. This series continues work that we began with Fontana Books, in their 'Political Issues' series. Some similarities will be obvious, particularly in our injunction to authors to write at the highest possible level of intelligence but to eschew all jargon and technicalities. Students of politics should accept, not worry, that they have a public role.

Bernard Crick and Patrick Seyd

AUTHOR'S PREFACE

The source material for *The Politics of Town Planning* has been collected over a number of years, during which time there have been many people whose help, direct and indirect, I must acknowledge.

To my academic colleagues, both staff and students, at the University of Birmingham, I owe a considerable debt of gratitude for having stimulated my thinking in town planning and planning history more than they could imagine.

I also acknowledge the help given at interviews with Lord Duncan-Sandys, the Rt. Hon. Peter Shore, MP and the Rt. Hon. John Silkin, MP. I am grateful to them for the courtesy of their time and their helpful observations on town planning and their place in it. (Mr Silkin helped me particularly in respect of his father, Lord Silkin.) In correspondence, the Rt. Hon. Sir Keith Joseph, MP kindly drew my attention to a paper he had earlier given to a Civic Trust Conference.

Sir Wilfred Burns, Chief Planner at the Department of the Environment, has kindly read and commented on certain passages, particularly those relating to contemporary planning questions.

To Professor Bernard Crick, general editor of the Series, I am indebted for help and guidance. Needless to say, however, the views I am presenting are my own and, unless so accredited in the chapter references, should not be attributed to anyone else.

A final word of thanks is due first to my daughter Shelagh who has helped me with the preparation of the Index; also to my secretary, Miss Sue Elias, who has typed my manuscript in impeccable style.

Gordon E. Cherry
Centre for Urban and Regional Studies
University of Birmingham
July 1981

INTRODUCTION

This book, which seeks to illustrate the political dimensions of British town planning throughout the twentieth century, has two main objectives. The first is to show how town planning, first as a movement and then as a State activity, took root and developed in ways deeply affected by a variety of social and cultural influences. We shall see that while the strategic aims of town planning, encountered in its academic discipline and in its professional ideology, retain a fair degree of consistency over time, the actual operation of town planning practice is in greater flux. This is because the activity of town planning, mediated through political processes and operated through a variety of institutional arrangements, responds and adapts to different expressions of political values and social preferences which change over time. Political ideas change in respect of town planning and the role of the State; during this century all three main political parties can claim to have had a major influence on the course of town planning events. This becomes clear as we recount the history of modern town planning through political action and the influence of politicians, both of local and central government.

The second objective is to learn from the historical developments so that we may more readily understand the nature of contemporary town planning and the political forces which are acting upon it. This obliges us to consider particularly the present state of the British planning system and its limitations in meeting, at all effectively, community aspirations and environmental objectives. The place of town planning in urban and regional governance is consequently examined.

This historical narrative begins in Chapter 1 where the factors surrounding the origins of modern town planning are described at the turn of the last century. The eight decades of this century are divided into two; Chapter 2 deals with the period to 1939 and Chapter 3 covers the years from 1940 to the present day. These chapters constitute a marked departure from conventional town planning histories, written in terms of professional achievements and the activities of professional practice. The political history cannot, of course, pretend to be complete; the research has not yet been done, and in any case the sheer volume and complexity of the war time and post-war Official Histories so far published suggest that it would not easily be condensed into one short book. But sufficient will be shown to indicate the main threads of the political dimension to date, and the circumstances in which they weave into the tapestry of our social affairs. These early chapters can be read almost as a history of town planning in a political context. But they are intended to be more than that, for they outline the history of the political controversy of this century as to whether there should be such a thing as town planning at all, and if so, what forms it should take. Planning was not something which followed from the existence of planners; rather it became an activity with political legitimation as a consequence of demand.

Chapter 4 summarises the political attitudes and convictions which have underpinned British town planning. We cannot claim to see any unified set of political doctrines, rather a number of separate and often contradictory political themes, which over a period of time, for widely differing reasons, have appealed to various individuals and groups. The strength with which these themes or convictions have been held has given an essential framework to town planning legislation and commitment to various courses of action.

Chapter 5 looks at planning and politics in practice: how the system actually works as a consequence of interactions within and between the three-fold elements – the political, the professional/ bureaucratic and actors in the community. Each part is illustrated with examples and shows the planning system at work. The chapter concludes with a review of recent planning issues, confirming planning as an interactive system in matters of housing, metropolitan strategies, regional planning, transportation, conservation and environmentalism.

Chapter 6 considers the major political questions before town planning today: its aims, its methods and the institutional forms of government through which as a State activity it becomes operative. It is timely to do this. Throughout this century until very recent years the State has considerably enlarged its hold on our community affairs. In the later 1970s there was evidence that in Britain, Western Europe and North America the seemingly inexorable trend was to be reversed. The future of town planning might be at a very interesting crossroads. Questions are raised as to how much planning will reside with the public sector, what forms of community planning can best be devised, at what levels of government these will be arranged, and whether town planning can be properly integrated into urban (and rural, and regional) management.

Chapter 7 examines the main conclusions of the political history and the contemporary political setting for town planning. This enables us to suggest a new set of approaches for academics, professionals, administrators and the community at large, which relate to the nature of the British planning system and its institutional framework. There are no suggestions as to the strategic directions of town planning policy, instead the focus is on the political dimensions of town planning practice, particularly at local level, and the ways in which the planning system needs modification if social preferences and general environmental objectives are going to be met.

For Margaret

Chapter one

TOWN PLANNING AND THE POLITICAL DIMENSION

TOWN PLANNING TODAY

Town planning is now a well known term. First used in 1906 (and in British legislation in 1909), it has entered into the language of governments the world over, and is now a distinctive academic and professional subject field, it affecting all of our lives. The ideas with which it has been associated have been exported to all continents; through them the State has sought to manage, guide and control the forces which shape and change our built environment. Ostensibly for community benefit (though the claim has not always been without challenge), restriction is placed on private action to develop land and erect buildings in order that the environment might reflect the intentions of public plans. Town planning has become an important weapon in the twentieth century armoury of State powers.

For an activity of such extent and importance, the term is surprisingly ambiguous. Indeed it has never been defined in British legislation, and there is a welter of other terminology which makes precise meaning obscure. This may be stimulating for academic debate but bewildering for the average citizen, so much so that it may be tempting to explain, albeit lamely, that 'town planning is what town planners do'.

Town planning was an adequate term so long as it meant town building, town design or the process of preparing schemes for town development. By and large this was the case in the first three decades of this century, but legislation in 1932 preferred the expression 'town and country', a phrase which presupposed an extension of subject content as well as a wider geographical scale of operation. Since then, a preference for latin rather than anglo-saxon has introduced 'urban and regional'. Meanwhile the Americans employ the term 'city planning'. Confusion is increased when 'planning' is applied to other subject matter. Land-use planning or physical planning is roughly synonymous to town and country planning in Britain, but other expressions such as transport-, health-, education-, recreation-, and tourism planning have distinct meanings related to their discrete subject areas. We may also speak of social and economic planning, but here the term refers to public policy in a range of related activities. Phraseology is made more complicated, however, with the use of the single word: 'planning' is now an overworked word (and 'planners' a journalistic shorthand almost devoid of meaning) though certainly it represents an activity which has expanded enormously this century as the tentacles of State involvement have reached into most corners of our lives. Indeed, we would probably agree that it represents one of the primary governmental features of our generation.

Used singly, planning is therefore a generic term. It may be described as purposive action designed to achieve a future situation or set of circumstances. It may embrace many fields of activity. But it is also a word which can be added to a subject area to give more precise definition. One of these areas is town planning, which geographically has come to embrace towns, cities, rural areas, countryside and regions; attempts to summarise this collection under the single heading 'environmental' usually causes more confusion than it is worth. At first, town planning was an activity which in broad terms aimed at securing the right use of land, and establishing control over the processes of development in order to secure qualitative improvements in the environment. We need to be a little more definitive than this, however. The difficulty is that the range of town planning does not remain constant, and any definition will change over time. Thus we need a historical perspective.

Contemporary town planning grew out of the experience gained, and the institutional structures established during the decades of Victorian urban management – those many years when British cities were lit, paved, drained and sewered and when the population was increasingly protected from the worst excesses of bad housing, poor sanitation and environmental squalor. This was the longer term context, but town planning was given its particular character by the perceived crisis of the late Victorian city and the remedies then put forward for its solution.[1] Britain was already an urban country as early as 1851 (the census then revealed that for the first time more than 50 per cent of the population was classed as urban), and not only London but also the growing towns of the industrial north and midlands presented urban living and working conditions, which increasingly fell to the State for improvement. The sanitary and related environmental hazards could reasonably be tackled through bye law control and health and other regulations. But one outstanding set of problems remained, and these related to housing.

The legacy of the nineteenth century was the accumulation of unfit dwellings, high overcrowding rates and the high residential densities in the big cities. Given also the endemic poverty stemming from low wages and irregular employment, the great challenge at the end of the century was the provision of working class accommodation: who should provide it, where it should be located, and at what rent? One solution was the building of cheap, cheery, salubrious houses on land in the suburbs, in association with the reform movements which stressed the importance of fresh air, space and sunlight. Low density housing with new forms of residential layout reflected these aims. The foundations of contemporary town planning were therefore laid: the purposeful selection of land for the protection of suburban house building according to new environmental and design criteria.

This early focus on housing provision (of a suitable kind, with an appropriate layout and location) has passed. But the core of British town planning retains its flavour: it can still be described essentially as an activity designed to secure the right use of land and to control, in the interests of the community, those myriad decisions to erect or change the use of buildings so as to guide the changing shape and structure of cities over time in accordance with a prepared plan. Modern town planning is a comprehensive exercise of analysis and prescription covering the regulation of environmental and community affairs far beyond its early remit. It is no longer simply a technical exercise of land selection and physical design. It has broadened into an activity of social purpose where the shaping of the physical environment is conducted within a web of social and economic objectives. Town planning, once seen as the product of the design professions – architecture and engineering – is now regarded just as much a social science.

Because of this, modern town planning is an activity which demands a thorough knowledge of those matters which bring about change in social and economic affairs. For example, there are demographic factors: birth rates, population structure (age and ethnicity), household formation and migration patterns; and social factors: changes in life styles and population preferences, in family structure and social relations, and in social values and attitudes, to be taken into account. Technological factors, innovations and scientific discovery also affect the environment and pose new social opportunities and challenges. Furthermore economic factors provide another area of change: rates of economic growth, structural changes in the economy, employment and unemployment, changing patterns of income distribution and consumption, and changes in work/time patterns. Finally, the social and economic environments are influenced through the institutions of government: the relative extent of involvement of the public sector, the fiscal policy, the political system, the instruments of government and the value systems of those instruments.

Town planning has therefore come to represent a means of public control over the development of towns, cities, their hinterlands and regions, and the adaptation of these to the changing conditions of modern life. Negatively it is concerned with the control of abuse and the regulation of those things considered harmful to the community; positively it represents social, economic and environmental policy to achieve certain aims unattainable through the unfettered operation of the private sector. It deals with the problems of contemporary urbanisation, not only remedying malfunction, but also creating the conditions for harmonious living. (Health, beauty and convenience have been long standing objectives in securing model cities.) It deals with the allocation of land for stated purposes; it seeks to relate economic planning to the physical structuring of cities; and it aims to enhance living conditions for the community as a whole.

THE POLITICAL CONTEXT

Town planning is undertaken by many actors. In Britain there is a planning profession (the Royal Town Planning Institute) whose members collectively represent the skills, expertise and proven competence in the subject field. There are of course other professional bodies engaged in related areas, and it would be unwise to draw demarcation lines too sharply between architects, engineers, land surveyors, landscape architects and others. All these professionals have been trained within a set of ideologies; they have their own ideas of ends or objectives which are right or wrong, desirable or undesirable, and they work towards these in ways which will gain them most credit from their peer group.

The civil servant also has an important role. British town planning represents a set of statutory obligations or permissive functions carried out by local government with powers provided by the central State. Local authorities draw up plans; central government approves them. The local government officer and the civil servant (they may or may not also be professionals) carry out their duties as bureaucrats within their own value systems: to defend the established order of which they are part, and to ensure that action takes place within recognised, correct procedures. Neither the professional nor the civil servant are by collective temperament radical; they are usually cautious and conservative. They defend interests, they protect systems. This is not to say that they are never innovative, rather that they constitute one of a number of checks or balances which by and large make for an evolutionary, adaptive governmental system.

The professional claims to serve society, the civil servant to serve the politician. In the British system of representative democracy, the elected politician takes public decisions. He obviously has his own political values, and political ideologies clearly have much to say about planning. In planned-economy countries, public intervention in land use is a matter of political philosophy. In other countries public intervention is held to conflict with the laws of the land market. Questions of public housing, regional development, forms of central area rebuilding, location of population, New Towns and a whole range of other matters within the field of town planning have become matters for political debate.

Thus town planning is a political activity. It is a function of government, and the people who operate the system (professionals, civil servants and politicians) inevitably subscribe to values and ideologies which have a bearing on decisions and policies. These are made in respect of other people; some will gain from a decision but some will lose. Town planning is political also in the sense that it is an allocative activity: it distributes rewards, resources and opportunities throughout the community. In a century which has claimed to move towards a more equal society, town planning has been one of the agents in that process. Furthermore, it is political in that there is a dialogue between planner and planned, governor and governed. The decision-making process in town planning is a complex web of interaction between institutional frameworks of government and external pressures from the community. Government rarely fails to be responsive to outside lobbies and pressure groups (although there may be serious lags in time for the strength of pressure to register), and in recent years there have been attempts to institutionalise these in public participation.

Town planning is thus a State activity which attempts to shape and guide the forces of environmental change. The ways in which it does this have been, and are, the subject of controversy. For example, it used to be fashionable to adopt a pluralist stance, explaining that the State was an intermediary, engaged in the management of competing demands of different groups and interests in society. The State was held to be neutral, guided by notions of fairness and equity in which favour was shown to none. A quite different view would be an instrumentalist stance, which holds that State policy corresponds with the interests of the dominant class. Consequently State policy is the instrument by which that dominance is maintained. Other views might adopt a structuralist stance. For example, with regard to economic affairs, State policy might seek to aid the profitability of a country; in other words the State would underpin national survival and permit the expansion of private industry in a mixed economy.

There will be a number of variations, but the adoption of any one in no way weakens the political dimension of town planning. Control over the use of land has become a major issue, both in cities and in the countryside, throughout the twentieth century. Indeed, since 1945 it has assumed very great importance. In a variety of ways, local authorities, central government and its quasi public agencies have sought to shape the spread and internal structure of cities, and to protect land from being built on at all. They have done this for social and economic reasons. But, as has been stated, benefits do not accrue to all, and there are differential gains and losses among various community groups. Even with this recognition, the situation is not straightforward in that the actual consequences of a planning strategy may be quite different from those intended. Take for example the post-war land-use policy of containing urban Britain, whereby its major cities were girded with Green Belts, and the population dispersed to satellites and New Towns. On the face of it this was planning for the least fortunate (the overcrowded, the ill housed, those most deprived of open space). But, as Peter Hall concludes, in practice the system has had a reverse effect: 'it is the most fortunate who have gained the most benefits from the operation of the system, while the least fortunate have gained very little.'[2]

Efforts to control development in accordance with a long-term plan are therefore intimately bound up with politics at central and local level. But the actual way in which politics will be exercised and articulated at various levels will depend on the forms of governmental structure which particular countries develop. In Britain we have to reflect on a history of 150 years or more, during which time we have experienced a remarkable extension of State intervention in society at both central and local levels. During the nineteenth century, the foundation of the modern civil service was laid, local government was reformed and a range of effective *ad hoc* bodies was created. After the years of Bentham's influence, a period of collectivism gradually superceded individualism. Public health and factory regulation were instances of mid-century legislation which were designed to have a major impact on individual behaviour in the belief that these controls would produce public benefit. The problems posed by urban industrial society necessarily enlarged the activities of the State: it was necessary to prevent things being done to people; unrestrained competition had consequences destructive of the general good. 'Gas and water municipal socialism' gave people experience of large scale public undertakings, and these proliferated in the twentieth century as the State began to provide services for people.

Fraser[3] has suggested a five-stage model of State growth, and this is helpful to an understanding of the political context which town planning has inherited. First there was the revelation of some evil which society came to view as intolerable (for example, the exploitation of children). Legislation was passed to prevent it. When this was found to be ineffective, inspectors were employed to ensure enforcement. New legislation was passed with stronger provisions, and new groups of professional people were recruited to further enforce it. In due time they themselves became lobbyists for increases in the powers of their agencies. Then came the recognition that the problems would require continuous regulation. Finally, an elaborate framework of law was developed with a complex bureaucratic machine to enforce it.

In the twentieth century this last stage has seen the burgeoning of State rules and regulations. The first town planning legislation (1909) carried fourteen sections covering nine pages. In 1975, the Parliamentary Statement of the Law relating to planning control over the development of land covered the contents of 35 Acts of Parliament and extended to 1231 pages of annotated statutory legislation, all to be read alongside a body of subordinate legislation comprising 171 statutory instruments covering 880 annotated pages.[4] The Town and Country Planning Act (1971) the seventeenth Act of its kind since 1909, carried no less than 295 sections and 25 schedules, covering 382 pages. The Local Government,

Planning and Land Act (1980) is scarcely less formidable, with 197 sections and 34 schedules, extending to 330 pages.

We should also note the growth in the machinery and manpower of central government, particularly around the end of the century. For example, Boards were created to take over functions performed earlier by the Privy Council and the Home Office: Local Government (1870), Agriculture (1889) and Education (1913). Meanwhile with civil service reform there was an expansion of government staff. In 1832 there were merely 21,300 civil servants in the UK; even in 1880 the figure was only 50,000, but in 1914 it was 280,000. Significant changes began to take place. In Central Government wider discretionary powers were given to Ministers and their Departments, and there was an extension of delegated legislation, particularly in the years before the First World War. At local level, the salaried official became increasingly important, at the expense of the influence of the local politician. Hennock reminds us that 'much of the financial success of the purchase of the gas works and the water works in the mid 70s, not to mention the Birmingham Improvement Scheme, was due to Joseph Chamberlain's skill as a negotiator.'[5] In the twentieth century the architect for the City's Inner Ring Road and the redevelopment of the old slum areas was the City Engineer and Planning Officer, Herbert Manzoni.

This illustrates the institutional context of town planning's development. Local government is of particular importance because, as we shall see, town planning depends very much on performance at individual local authority level for its reception by the community whose interests are supposed to be served. For most of the period under review we are concerned with boroughs and county councils. The boroughs were created by the Municipal Corporations Act (1835), although for a long time they were regarded as trustees of public property rather than as providers of social services. The county councils were created in 1888, taking over certain functions previously the responsibility of the Quarter Sessions. Until 1894 there was an array of special bodies such as burial boards, local boards of health, lighting inspectors, commissioners of baths and wash-houses, and highway boards; with some exceptions they were then consolidated into urban and rural districts and parish councils. The London County Council was created in 1889, superceding the Metropolitan Board of Works.

By the beginning of the twentieth century, local authorities were well established; they provided sanitary services, police and highway maintenance, and some went much further, with responsibilities for water, gas, electricity, trams, buses, libraries, cemeteries and docks. Moreover, the principle of local inspection was accepted in fields of poor law, public health, education and police. For example, engineering inspectors held local inquiries related to the development of local sewerage systems. The significance of this is that town planning found itself naturally rooted in a local government structure, and the inspection system incorporated in the first Act of 1909 had proven experience.

There was a growing belief in the efficacy and strengths of local government. This was to be of great significance for town planning. For example, Joseph Chamberlain believed that

the most fruitful field before reformers at the present time is to be found in an extension of the functions and authority of local government. Local government is near the people. Local government will bring you into contact with the masses. By its means you will be able to increase their comforts, to secure their health, to multiply the luxuries which they may enjoy in common, to carry out a vast cooperate system for mutual aid and support, to lessen the inequalities of our social system, and to raise the standard of all classes in the community. I believe that in this way you may help to equalise to a great extent the condition of men, and to limit the extremes which now form so great a blot on our social system.[6]

This emphasis (in 1885) on the capacity of the local State to be so benevolent in human affairs held sway for many years. His son, Neville Chamberlain, as Minister of Health, more than 40 years later (in 1929), could declare: 'local government comes so much nearer to the homes, and therefore to the hearts of people, than any national government can. To them it is something friendly, something familiar, something accessible. ... They look to it because it has ideals which they understand, and that they approve, and because it is always helping and teaching them to rise to higher things.'[7]

How different are the sentiments today! But during the years in question the emergent local government machine produced an acceptable and workable fulcrum for town planning. As Fraser remarks: 'by 1885 ... English urban authorities had become institutions with wide social purposes, and they really did conduce to the general welfare of the local community.'[8] The municipal revolution of 1835 took time to be effective, but this was a noticeable consequence. Town planning found a ready mould in local government and local politics.

The politics of town planning

Given this decidedly political context and the importance of the institutional framework of government for British town planning activity, it would be reasonable to claim to see some explanations for town planning this century in political and institutional terms. It will, however, always be debatable how far political considerations can explain town planning developments. We know that there are many actors influencing events: professional, bureaucrat and politician, all interacting with a host of external and other factors; and that most events will therefore be extremely complex in both their origins and evolution. But at least we can recognise some political dimension of explanation present in most cases.

It will be helpful to admit two levels of explanation. One will be macro in scale, illustrating a political situation at any one point in time in respect of the balance of forces which represent the interests and values of those groups in a position to exercise power or control over others. Another will be micro, showing the part played by individuals in a political role in respect of particular town planning questions. The individual politician acts in the context of the general political situation at the time; he may act in accordance with it, or not, but he always has the ability to break through a particular web of circumstances and so make a personal mark on events.

Subsequent chapters in this book will give examples of the political voice in the story of town planning. The broader political situation will also be described. But for the remainder of this chapter we can usefully confirm the nature of the political dimension with the example of those twenty formative years which saw the origins of modern town planning.

There is ample evidence of the poverty of health, housing and environmental conditions in the late Victorian city. The population of Birmingham for example, in the 1880s, had a life expectancy at birth of forty three years, 45 per cent of deaths were children under the age of five, and 43 per cent were attributable to seven major groups of air-, water-, and food-borne diseases.[9] There were plenty of commentators on the urban crisis. Jack London (author about life in the Klondike) came to London in 1902, lived near the docks for two months and in *The People of the Abyss* (1903), wrote about the wretchedness of urban conditions. Charles Chaplin in *My Autobiography* (1966), describes entering the Lambeth workhouse; he had been born in 1889 at Walworth and grew up in Lambeth and elsewhere south of the river. Robert Roberts in *The Classic Slum* (1971), describes his early life at a corner shop in one of the poorest parts of Salford before the First World War.

Well before this, however, housing conditions had become a target for protest literature of a vivid kind. *The Bitter Cry of Outcast London* (1883), portrayed the squalor of urban living; it was a short but sharp pamphlet commonly ascribed to the Secretary of the London Congregational Union, the Rev. Andrew Mearns. A survey undertaken by the Social Democratic Foundation described the incidence of poverty for *The Pall Mall Gazette* (1885). Poverty was also a feature in Charles Booth's seventeen volumes of *Life and Labour of the People in London* (1889 *et seq.*). General William Booth of the Salvation Army pointed to the abject living conditions of the 'submerged tenth' of the population in *In Darkest England and the Way Out* (1890). Seebohm Rowntree's *Poverty: a Study of Town Life* (1901), changed the focus to a provincial city, revealing that York's population was experiencing poverty on a scale comparable to that of London.

The facts of housing deprivation were also well known.[10] Overcrowding and density was revealed in Census records. In 1901 no less than 16 per cent of the population of London (the Administrative County) was classed as overcrowded, the term defined as more than two persons per room. Finsbury (35%), Stepney (33%), Shoreditch and Bethnal Green (30% each) were boroughs within London which recorded very high overcrowding rates. Elsewhere in England, the north east with similar proportions was also notoriously overcrowded. With an accompanying lack of open space, it followed that high population density figures obtained, and pockets of exceptional densities occurred in certain districts of London and the larger cities. Together with insanitary housing, a shortage of accommodation for the working classes, low wages, and insecure employment, these conditions became a target for a variety of reform measures.

Housing reform had long been promoted through the building of alternative model housing by private, philanthropic benefactors, and towards the end of the century in the form of model estates, of which Bournville, created by George Cadbury in Birmingham, is a classic example. The extent of these provisions could in no way meet demand, however, and attention turned increasingly to the promise of local authority building, though before the First World War only London achieved any scale of enterprise. Land reform also had its adherents. High land values in the central districts of cities were held to be a chief cause of poor housing conditions; land nationalisation was advocated by some, while others, following Henry George, the economist, favoured a new kind of land tax. Further, a strategy for population redistribution was increasingly supported in the context of the creation of garden cities; Ebenezer Howard's *Tomorrow: a peaceful path to real reform* (1898), (reissued with amendments as *Garden Cities of Tomorrow* (1902)) was particularly influential.

Embracing all these reform movements was the need for social reform, an overriding concern being the moral consequences of bad housing and environmental conditions. Reformers saw a close connection between environment and social response. Typical (but outstanding) was the work of Canon and Mrs Barnett. In 1909 they could nicely compare their creation of Hampstead Garden Suburb with the older housing areas of East London where there were 'no gardens, no trees, no open spaces, no public buildings, no children's playgrounds, no spacious thoroughfares, no broad, shady roads, the whole stamped by the landlord's greed, the builder's competition, and the people's helplessness.'[11] Canon Barnett had worked for twenty years in the East End as vicar of St Jude's, Whitechapel, and later as Warden of Toynbee Hall. His concern was not so much with specific social problems but with the whole context of urban social life. He sought to establish better norms for urban living and these he described for the citizens of Bristol in *The Ideal City* (1893), when he was appointed a Canon of Bristol Cathedral.[12]

Most cities had their housing reform lobbies. Sheffield , for example, had an Association for the Better Housing of the Poor, and in the 1890s, with the cooperation of the Sheffield Trades Council, formed a pressure group on the town council. Manchester had an energetic Citizens' Association, which carried out an impressive housing survey in 1904. But the focus was London and at the end of the century we may reasonably summarise the situation as follows. An early solution of the working class housing problem seemed remote: high land values and low rates of return made it an unlikely area for the private sector; private philanthropy could not do much more than it had already achieved; and there was strong political resistance to the argument that local authorities themselves should build houses on sufficient scale. Therefore the immediate answer seemed to be the building of cheaper houses by the private sector in the suburbs, and a consequent 'filtering up' of housing quality in the older areas. New suburban building offered the attractions of fresh air, space and sunlight. By the end of the century an outward movement of population from the big cities to the suburbs was already occurring, and indeed in Greater London the areas showing the fastest population growth in Britain were the suburbs of East Ham, Walthamstow, Willesden and Hornsey. Given this situation, we can place the first Town Planning Act in the context of its time; its significance was that it gave permissive powers to local authorities to make town planning schemes for land in course of development. The general origins of modern town planning in Britain were provided by housing and social reform; more particularly they were the conditions surrounding the late Victorian housing crisis, especially in London in relation to the housing of the working classes.

We can now consider the related political context. Foster shows that the London housing crisis was of some magnitude.[13] Rents had risen throughout the second half of the century and by 1900 were above a quarter of the average working class budget. Ground values and rents were much higher than for a normal industrial city. Wages were rising only slowly. Investment overseas was attractive and the flow of money into domestic housing diminished, being no longer profitable. Economic difficulties deriving from seasonal employment, trade depression and housing problems underlay the riots of February 1886 which followed the East End rent strikes of 1883–84.

The legalisation of trade union activity and the widening of the franchise in 1867 and 1884 considerably increased the potential bargaining power of labour. Furthermore the introduction of universal elementary education after 1870 and the growth of a popular press illustrated the widening democratic base of society. But the trades unions were weak and political power resided elsewhere; London elected 72 Members of Parliament and its rents formed much of the collective fortune of the House of Lords. The Tories captured the majority of the capital's seats for two decades after 1884. In Labour politics the marxist Social Democratic Foundation, not the Fabian inspired trade union leaders, was dominant, and when the SDF ran out of steam, London's Labour Party became established in the first decade of the twentieth century.

This confirms the importance of reconstructing the political context within which State power is exercised at any one time. It seems reasonable to argue that London's housing crisis reached its dimensions towards the end of the century precisely because the political balance of forces at that time was not conducive to securing the changes that were needed. Edwardian Britain and the years of the reforming Liberal Government broke the deadlock. Important changes had taken place in Liberalism, and the mid-Victorian *laissez faire* attitude gave way to moral and social reform.

Adopted forms of town planning therefore do not simply 'occur'. Neither can town planning be regarded solely as the product of enlightenment: a natural, altruistic response to intolerable conditions. Nor is it necessarily the product of the development of professional skills. These matters are important, but we should first look at the context in which they are grounded. I have argued that political and related institutional influences help to explain particular directions of change. This is the political dimension of town planning. In the next chapters I shall discuss the political circumstances surrounding the development of town planning in this century.

Chapter two

DEVELOPMENTS IN TOWN PLANNING – PRE-1939

THE 1909 ACT

Towards the end of the nineteenth century there was, as we have seen, increasing pressure for housing reform. But there was insufficient political pressure to secure reform through legislation. In the first decade of the twentieth century, however, the party political balance changed, and the first Town Planning Act dates from this time.

An important early influence came not from London but Birmingham. The city already had a tradition of effective and enterprising municipal government, highlighted by the achievements of Joseph Chamberlain's mayorality in the 1870s. Local Unitarians and Quakers, active in their concern for social questions, maintained a stream of continuity in the town's corporate life. Unitarian mayors held office almost without break between 1840 and 1880, and Unitarian families such as the Chamberlains and Nettlefolds occupied important positions in local business. In the 1890s George Cadbury had begun a nationally renowned housing development at Bournville, of a form which contrasted sharply with the bye law streets of adjoining Selly Oak. Circumstances were propitious for other housing reform initiatives and social reform received a fillip with the arrival of Bishop Gore from Worcester in 1905, as the first Bishop of the City.

The city's housing and social problems were acute. The Medical Officer of Health's Annual Reports repeatedly emphasised the problem of the central districts with high mortality rates and enormously high and expensive sickness rates. In 1901, the *Birmingham Daily Gazette* sent a special correspondent to report on local conditions in the slums; his findings, very much in the tradition of late nineteenth century protest literature, were reprinted in *Scenes in*

Slumland (1902). Although it took some time to become apparent, the overcrowding in central Birmingham had in fact reached its peak and was beginning to decline appreciably. Between 1896 and 1911, the number of occupied houses in the twelve innermost wards fell by nearly 10 per cent, while the number in the six outer wards rose by 30 per cent. A process of suburbanisation followed, and this extended into the surrounding counties of Staffordshire, Warwickshire and Worcestershire. There was a significant displacement and redistribution of population, which followed the pattern established in London over the last three decades of the century, when the population of the outer rings increased substantially.

In 1901, a new Housing Committee of the Council was established. This was created out of the old Estates and Health Committees. The proposal was bitterly contested, as reflected by the close voting, 32 to 30. The new Committee assumed all powers exercised under the Housing Acts and such powers under the Public Health Acts as might be thought desirable. Councillor J. S. Nettlefold, member for Edgbaston-Harborne Ward since 1898, became Chairman, and over the next few years developed a coherent policy based on provision for private building in the suburbs, compulsion of owners to repair their property, avoidance of large scale demolition and a continuing hostility towards municipal house building.

John Sutton Nettlefold was born in London in 1866.[1] He came to Birmingham at the age of twelve and entered the local offices of Nettlefold and Co. He worked for a time in South Wales when he married Margaret, the daughter of Arthur Chamberlain. On his return to Birmingham he was elected to the City Council in 1898 at the age of thirty two. His chairmanship of the new Housing Committee enabled him to wield an extraordinary influence. His housing policies were soon stated; first in 1902 (largely for financial reasons), against municipal house building. The Housing of the Working Classes Act (1900) extended to provincial boroughs the powers given to London in 1890, important amongst which was the power to establish lodging houses outside their own districts. Lodging houses had already been defined to include separate cottages and tenements for the working classes, and so in effect the boroughs now possessed powers to build houses not only on land cleared through town improvement schemes but on other suitable land as well. Moreover, the Act was interpreted as giving powers to build, not merely rebuild, for the poor; up to this time legislation had been seen as giving powers only for the rehousing of people displaced through slum clearance. Nettlefold stood out against the growing support for local authority house building for the working classes; other aspects of his housing (and later, town planning) policies were partly consequential upon this. He clearly reflected the popular local view, for in spite of the great need to increase the supply of good cheap houses in the city there was little support for municipal building. Towards the end of the nineteenth century, two blocks of houses were erected by the Corporation, and later, there was another scheme, but there the contribution rested.

By 1905, there was evidence that Nettlefold had been influenced by T. C. Horsfall, a Manchester housing reformer, whose advocacy of municipal development on the lines of German municipalities had been published in 1904 (*The Example of Germany*). In a small pamphlet on housing policy, Nettlefold quoted from Horsfall, recommending the laying out of large tracts of land on a comprehensive plan with a sufficient number of broad streets, playgrounds and open space. His town planning ideas were stimulated by an official visit to a number of German towns in the summer of 1905. A Report later that year noted the outstanding features which had been observed: the town expansion plan, the cost of streets and parks, land purchase, municipal house building, ownership of houses by working men, public encouragement to private enterprise in housing the working classes, house inspection, and the question of flats as opposed to single houses.

A fuller Report in 1906 made a plea for a 'complete consistent policy for dealing with the housing conditions in Birmingham'. The following extracts are particularly interesting:

The creation of new congested districts without the necessaries of healthy life now going on in large cities can only be prevented so far as our own City is concerned by obtaining power to forbid the erection of any new buildings except in accordance with a general plan for developing all uncovered land within the City boundaries.

Your Committee are of opinion that a Corporation cannot own too much land, provided that it is judiciously purchased. Municipal land could be laid out with open spaces and all other essentials to a healthy, happy community, with the additional advantage that any future rise in the value of land would directly or indirectly go to the ratepayers. The Corporation could then assist private individuals and Public Utility Building Societies, with whose bona fides they were satisfied, to erect at the lowest possible rate healthy cheerful houses for people with small incomes. The policy of buying land and encouraging other people to build the houses would enable the Corporation to give a great stimulus to the supply of good, cheap houses on the outskirts of the city, and would thereby benefit a very large number of people. It is now universally recognised to be of the utmost importance to spread the populations of our large cities over a greater area than hitherto, and your Committee are convinced that public money spent on land purchase would effect far more towards the solution of the Housing problem than money spent in any other way. . . . This policy of the Municipality creating ground rents, and directing the development of building land, on sound, sanitary, and cheerful lines, has worked most successfully in Germany from the hygenic point of view, without putting a charge on the rates which all classes have to bear directly or indirectly.

The Report went on to explain that in order to enforce Town Expansion plans, and to carry out a vigorous policy of land purchase, fresh legislation was essential: an expression of opinion in favour of such general legislation would assist the passage of a Bill through Parliament.

In presenting his Report, Nettlefold made a lengthy speech which was well received. His distinctive ideas about town planning were emerging: 'The Garden City idea, the Garden Suburb idea, have taken hold of the minds of Englishmen' he declared. 'We cannot hope to make Birmingham into a Garden City, although something can be done towards that end, but we can, if we will, create Garden Suburbs around Birmingham.' The relationship between housing and town planning was further emphasised: 'The home of the individual is the most important factor in the prosperity of the nation, and the strength of the Empire. We can, if we will, arrange for healthy, wholesome surroundings for every Birmingham adult, and, even more important, give every Birmingham child light and fresh air which is so essential to its healthy development.'

Council resolved in favour of Nettlefold's motion for legislation – the first local authority to do so. A year later a Conference of Local Authorities on Town Planning held at Manchester brought the matter before the Association of Municipal Corporations (AMC). Nettlefold was Chairman of the Town Planning Committee of AMC, and the Association prepared a scheme for a draft Bill. A deputation from AMC went to the Prime Minister and the President of the Local Government Board, and they were promised that the matter would receive earnest and sympathetic attention. Thus developed the chain of events following Birmingham's deputation to Germany and Nettlefold's grasp of town planning and its relevance to the situation in Britain.

Circumstances for legislation were propitious because of the changing political scene. There was both an increasing tension in society and a commitment to reform. On the one hand was the fear of German militarism, the struggle for women's suffrage, employment problems, the Irish question and the fear of anarchy, but on the other, there was an alertness to the need for reform. This was promoted not least by the knowledge that something like a third of the population lived in conditions of degradation. It was significant that during the Boer War a large proportion of those enlisting for service in Queen Victoria's army were found to be unfit. The Inter-Departmental Committee on Physical Deterioration, set up by the Government in 1903, recognised that the degeneration of the city populace had led to reduced labour efficiency.

The political possibility of reform came with a brilliant flowering of Liberal power in the Governments of Sir Henry Campbell-Bannerman and H. H. Asquith, following the Liberal Party land-slide victory of 1906. The twentieth-century welfare state took early recognisable form with legislation such as the Education Provision of Meals) Act (1906); the Education (Administrative Provisions) Act (1907), which made it a duty of a local authority to provide for the medical inspection of children; the Unemployed Workmen Act (1907); the Old Age Pensions Act (1908); and the Labour Exchanges Act (1909). These were the years which saw the publication of the young W. H. Beveridge's *Unemployment, a Problem of Industry* (1909), and the introduction of National Insurance (1911). It was in this period also that town planning legislation was first initiated. The Minister was John Burns, but his contribution should not be over-emphasised as the Hampstead Garden Suburb Act (1906), which conferred powers on the Hampstead Garden Suburb Trust 'to develop and lay out lands as garden suburbs', was already a model for national legislation.

Burns, brought up in humble circumstances, was born in Lambeth in 1858.[2] From the mid 1870s onwards he was a familiar orator in Battersea Park and Clapham Common. He stood as an Independent Labour Candidate in the General Election of 1886, but achieved greater notoriety in his organisation of the great Dock Strike in 1889. In 1892, he was elected MP for Battersea under the auspices of the Battersea Labour League. Over a period of time, his radical ideas faded and he broke with Keir Hardie. In 1905, he became President of the Local Government Board. He gained the reputation of an egotist, a bombast and a vain showman. But as the first working man to enter a Cabinet, his background was surely significant for developments in town planning. As he remarked many years later (1931), 'I was born in a slum and this made me a town planner. Having slept in Windsor Castle and Pentonville I think I am an authority on housing.'[3]

In November 1906, the National Housing Reform Council organised a deputation to the Prime Minister (Campbell-Bannerman) and Burns, and submitted a programme of housing and town planning legislation.[4] The deputation was led by an alderman on the Richmond (Surrey) town council, William Thompson, and a party of sixteen included George Cadbury and the Bishop of Wakefield. They advocated a number of reforms covering housing and public health, the creation of model suburbs, a simplified procedure for the compulsory purchase of land, a Town and Village Development Commission, the availability of cheaper money and town extension planning.

As with Nettlefold's delegation, the Prime Minister pledged that legislation would be introduced as soon as circumstances permitted, and a Bill was introduced in 1908. It fell considerably short of the deputation's hopes and was simply a short second part of a longer piece of legislation dealing chiefly with housing. Its object was: 'to ensure, by means of schemes which may be prepared either by local authorities or landowners, that in future, land in the vicinity of towns shall be developed in such a way as to secure proper sanitary conditions, amenity and convenience in connection with the laying out of the land itself and of any neighbouring land.'

Politicians of all parties may have been sympathetic to the ideals of town planning as expressed by reformers at Hampstead, Letchworth, Bournville, Earswick and the like, but the idea of extending municipal power over private interest was far too radical for many. Interference with the rights of private owners was, and continued to be, a major stumbling block.

The Housing, Town Planning etc. Bill had its First Reading in March 1908.[5] The housing part aimed to encourage house building (with cheap, fixed interest loans) in both urban and rural areas, adopting the provisions of the Housing of the Working Classes Act (1890). The town planning part aimed to secure greater coordination in the development of the land by encouraging local authorities and landowners to plan future developments through Planning Schemes, which once adopted, would become mandatory on developers to adhere to them. Any landowner would be able to claim compensation for loss of value due to the Scheme, but conversely a local authority would have power to collect 100 per cent of betterment accruing to a site as a result of a Scheme. The Bill included no powers to enable municipalities to buy land on their urban fringes (as reformers had been advocating) and it did not make town planning a mandatory activity for local authorities.

John Burns began his speech rather pompously: the aims of the Bill were 'to secure the home healthy, the house beautiful, the town pleasant, the city dignified and the suburb salubrious. It seeks and hopes to secure more houses, better houses, prettier streets, so that the character of a great people in towns and cities and villages can be still further improved and strengthened by the conditions under which they live.' The Bill was generally welcomed, but it stayed in Committee for twenty three days, until just a short time before the end of the Parliamentary Session. It was withdrawn with the promise that it would be brought forward at the start of the new session and considered in shortened procedure in a Committee of the whole House.

The Second Reading debate for what was now the 1909 Bill started in April. There was still a measure of accord for it both inside and outside the House. *The Builder*, for example, (11 September 1909) thought it 'a strong Bill drawn up by a strong man who wants something done'. But Conservatives baulked at the proposals for central control by the Local Government Board, and difficulties were apparent at the Committee stage when over 360 amendments were tabled. A strong attack came on the LGB: particularly its idea that inquiries should be held without legal trappings and its competence to decide planning matters. One opponent commented: 'Have we really come to this, that the Radical party, not content with legislating for every conceivable ill in the universe, are now coming down to say that the land owning class are not fit to be trusted to say whether or not they may employ counsel?'

When the Bill went to the Lords in September the opposition centred once again on the bureaucracy implied by town planning, as well as the problems surrounding claims for compensation. Earl Cawdor launched a grand attack, though the Bishop of Birmingham joined the Archbishop of Canterbury in speaking of its beneficial objectives. The Bill was returned to the Commons in November, and the Government remained firm on the point that the Local Government Board should oversee town planning. Burns claimed that 'if we are to save some local authorities from land speculation ... the action of a strong central authority is needed in the interests of public probity.' On the other hand the Government was prepared to compromise on compensation.

The Lords met to receive the Commons' comments. A 50 per cent betterment levy was agreed, and it was conceded that Schemes would not become law until they had laid on the Table of the two Houses for thirty days, during which time either House could object, in which case the Scheme became null and void. In later years this requirement was seen as a cumbersome delay. The Lords passed the Bill, but its teeth had been drawn. A week later the Government fell when the Lords refused to pass Lloyd George's Finance Act.

In retrospect it is surprising that the Act met with much success. In fact it was Birmingham that took up the permissive planning powers of the 1909 Act with singular enthusiasm; no other local authority in the country can match its record. The city's work between 1910 and 1914 was of major significance for the Local Government Board for the experience it needed in town planning practice. The Act met Birmingham's needs; Birmingham proceeded to show what could be done. The first application received by the Local Government Board for authority to prepare a scheme came from Birmingham – in respect of 2320 acres comprising the whole of the parish of Quinton and parts of the parishes of Harborne, Edgbaston and Northfield. By 1914, this and three other Schemes were waiting to be developed: East Birmingham, North Yardley and South Birmingham. By 1919, of the 13 schemes submitted to the Board, five (including an amending scheme) had been prepared by Birmingham.

Nettlefold left the City Council and became very critical not only of the 1909 Act and Birmingham's Schemes but also of the Local Government Board, which he thought 'so steeped in old and out of date methods that it has entirely failed to grasp the new situation created by town planning legislation.'[6] But in that city the baton passed to his half cousin, Neville Chamberlain, who became Chairman of a newly created Town Planning Committee. Before the outbreak of war his Committee was already considering the preparation of a Town Plan covering the whole built-up area of the city, foreshadowing developments of concept and practice which marked the 1920s.

THE 1919 ACT

The circumstances for the further development of town planning changed with the Great War and its aftermath. During the war years 'war socialism' meant a considerable extension of the role of Central Government; it was marked in such areas as price control, rent control and control over certain industries, but its incidence was haphazard and failed to provide any coherent strategy. More important were the years of planning for reconstruction, beginning in 1916 with an informal group of powerful heads of Departments working with the Prime Minister. Lloyd George's own Reconstruction Committee followed in 1917, and the same year saw a Ministry of Reconstruction. Continuing study on commercial and industrial policy, local government and housing proved fertile ground for town planning.

The creation of a Ministry of Health (in which town planning matters resided) in 1919, combined the duties of the Local Government Board and the Health Insurance Commissioners. Housing was an immediate priority. There was by this time a desperate shortage of dwellings, and the report of the Royal Commission on the Housing of the Industrial Population of Scotland (1917) was a reminder of the backlog of sub-standard housing north of the Border. The case for State provision of housing through the local authorities was now overwhelming, and political speeches on the 'homes for heroes' theme struck a powerful chord. Moreover, the threat of bolshevism abroad prompted fear of industrial unrest at home. Social pacification through improved housing provision was a clear antidote. Sir John Tudor Walters' report (for the Local Government Board) on building construction and provision of dwellings for the working classes was published in 1918. This laid down new housing standards which were sufficiently advanced to stand for a quarter of a century. In addition to this, far reaching recommendations were adopted covering such matters as density, site planning and house design. Meanwhile, propogandist groups for garden cities were active and Ebenezer Howard began the development of Welwyn in 1920.

Town planning legislation was once again an appendage of housing. As we shall see later, the Housing, Town Planning, etc. Act (1919), made it obligatory for local authorities to prepare surveys of their housing needs and to draw up plans for dealing with them; to all intents and purposes it introduced the council house and the inter-war council estate. The town planning part of the legislation similarly extended the role of the State, by making Scheme preparation compulsory for local authorities above a certain size (20,000 population), but even then only in respect (as with the 1909 Act) of land in course of development.

A Coalition Government was formed in January 1919, with Lloyd George as Prime Minister. Dr Christopher Addison (Liberal MP for Shoreditch), the first Minister of Health, presented his Bill in March.[7] The need for new housing measures was imperative and town planning gained from this favourable relationship. As

Addison remarked during the Second Reading (April) everyone would agree that it was necessary to provide new houses 'in a proper, far-sighted manner, that town planning has come to stay, and that we ought to encourage in the preparation of those schemes the use of the best talent that the country can provide.'

As presented, the Bill did not make town planning compulsory. Addison remarked that 'we ought to be very, very careful before we make town planning compulsory and see that we do not provide something which has an effect which may be quite indirect and quite unlooked for, but which may be very injurious to the development of housing'. But L. F. Scott (later Lord Justice Scott), a Coalition Conservative, quoted current French proposals for obligatory town planning, and when the Bill was committed to Standing Committee there was pressure for the Bill to go further than it did. Godfrey Locker-Lampson, another Coalition Conservative, introduced a new clause for compulsory town planning, attempting at first to make it obligatory for urban local authorities of 10,000 population and above, but later agreed to 20,000. Other attempts to widen the scope of legislation failed, for example proposals to extend town planning to the replanning of existing areas and to permit the appointment of regional planning committees.

The Bill, as amended, was considered in May. The new 'compulsory' clause was criticised but the Minister held firm and the clause stood. The Bill passed its Third Reading and came back from the Lords with certain amendments; with regard to town planning the population level of 20,000 now applied to rural districts as well as urban districts. The Royal Assent followed on 31 July. A Scottish Act entered the statute book shortly afterwards.

Town planning, however, was still not in any way a major political matter, being completely overshadowed by housing questions. But the relation between housing reform and town planning remained obvious and kept alive a movement for land use control which might otherwise have become sterile. Sir John Tudor Walters, a Coalition Liberal, made the point during the Second Reading: 'Do not let us set to work to fill up all the little bits of spaces in the centre of our towns with badly planned small houses. Let us go right out into the suburbs of our towns and cities; let us have belts of new housing schemes round our towns, planned and laid out on lines that are spacious and generous in their conception and in their execution.'

And so during the 1920s, statutory town planning entered a new phase. Scheme preparation now had a simpler set of procedures and by the end of the decade town planning, which might at the beginning have been regarded simply as a means of providing an orderly setting for new housing development, could be recognised as a wider local authority instrument of comprehensive land use control. The Chief Planning Adviser at the Ministry, George Pepler, encouraged and cajoled local authorities to prepare Schemes, but even then progress was very slow and in no way is it realistic to speak of compulsory town planning. The majority of local authorities failed to participate; certainly the shortage of qualified staff was a difficulty, but there were political stumbling blocks, including both apathy and opposition in principle, and the problem of dealing effectively with compensation and betterment seemed intractable.

THE 1932 ACT

The Town Planning Act of 1925 was a consolidating measure, but by the end of that decade there was pressure for new legislation. This came from the direction of a new, influential lobby founded in 1926: the Council for the Preservation of Rural England (CPRE), (Councils for Wales and Scotland followed shortly after). The CPRE was a joint initiative of Professor Patrick Abercrombie in his year as President of the Town Planning Institute and Guy Dawber, President of the Royal Institute of British Architects, together with the Earl of Crawford and Balcarres, then chairman of the Fine Arts Commission. The Council soon recruited some key influential figures and proved to be a powerful lobby for the preservation of countryside amenities, increasingly at risk from neglect or despoliation by unplanned development. In 1929, Sir Edward Hilton-Young, a Conservative Private Member, introduced a Rural Amenities Bill, designed to extend planning powers to rural land.

In that year, however, politics took a new course with the election of a majority Labour Government. An enhanced state role in community affairs might have been anticipated, and from a town planning perspective there were soon some interesting initiatives. For example, the Prime Minister, Ramsay Macdonald, set up a committee, chaired by Christopher Addison, the former Minister of Health, to consider the case for National Parks. In 1930, Arthur Greenwood's Housing Act introduced a shift in housing policies, providing for slum clearance and the rehousing of displaced families under subsidy arrangements. There were implications for urban replanning which required a new town planning Bill.

Greenwood's Town and Country Planning Bill (1931), super-ceded Hilton-Young's earlier proposals.[8] It was presented as a logical step in the elaboration of planning powers which had begun in 1909, attending now to slum clearance and extra housing provision. Planning powers would be extended to built up areas, and local authorities would be able to collect 100 per cent of the betterment generated by their planning schemes. It met with a surprising general approval. Neville Chamberlain remarked that 'there is much in this Bill which undoubtedly might have been the subject of a Bill brought in by the Conservatives'. Ernest Simon for the Liberals thought it a 'measure of enduring value to the country'. Hilton-Young wished the measure 'Godspeed'. Not everyone was so enthusiastic, however. The Marquis of Hartington hoped that 'there was one lesson the leaders of my party had learned, and that was that playing around with this kind of half-baked, pale pink socialism brings no good either to themselves or to the country'. The Bill passed through Standing Committee with little modification (although significantly the betterment charge was reduced to 75 per cent), but it went no further for in August a National Government was formed.

The General Election of October 1931, returned an overwhelmingly Conservative Parliament. The Labour Party was reduced to 52 MPs. Many new Members were pledged to cut back drastically public spending and to support measures which would restore public confidence and ease a desperate financial situation. There was little stomach for an interventionary State role and town planning stood little chance in a political climate which rejected interference in the operation of the private market.

The Bill was reintroduced, however, in 1932. Hilton Young was now Minister of Health and Chamberlain was Chancellor of the Exchequer; both were supporters of town planning. Introducing the Bill the Minister began with the hopeful claims that it was 'to a very large extent uncontroversial' and 'wholly non-partisan.'[9] Sir Stafford Cripps approved the Bill on behalf of the Labour Party: 'The general principle of the measure is in accord with what we believe to be the best social practice.' But the Tories would have none of it. Sir Derek Walker-Smith thought it 'just the kind of measure that a Socialist government would introduce' and objected to the power and control over property rights which was vested in local authority and government departments. Lord Hartington objected to giving power to local authorities because they were 'the greatest offenders and have been guilty of wholesale vandalism'. He preferred to use voluntary bodies, such as the CPRE.

In Standing Committee the Bill was fiercely attacked, and weakened. Betterment (nominally 75 per cent) was made virtually impossible to collect by restrictive clauses, while provisions for compensation were equally unsatisfactory. Town planning was once more made a permissive function of local authorities, and while the powers were supposed to apply to all types of land, the idea of exempt 'static areas' was introduced. A very powerful private property lobby secured the emasculation of the Bill, which received the Royal Assent in July 1932. Greenwood bitterly reflected: 'this Bill has been butchered to make a holiday for the diehard Tories. Their hostility is to the whole principle of town planning.'[10]

There was gloom and alarm in professional circles and it must have seemed that town planning faced an uncertain future. However, political and other events conspired to keep town planning alive at local and national levels and by the end of the decade a different set of circumstances promised a new outlook.

OTHER INITIATIVES

It would be wrong to think that the political planning history of the years between the wars was made solely by two town planning Acts. Politicians at both national and local levels made their mark on the tide of events, quite outside the scope of legislation.

In central Government Neville Chamberlain built on his Birmingham experience. At the age of fifty his life was to change dramatically when he was elected to Parliament, as Member for Ladywood. In his very first year Christopher Addison appointed him Chairman of a newly established Unhealthy Areas Committee, set up to consider the principles to be adopted in the clearance of slum areas.[11] Its Interim Report, submitted in March 1920, considered the particular problem of London. It concluded that there were only two alternative methods of relieving London's congestion: either by building high or by removing part of the population elsewhere and so achieving lower densities with large open spaces. The second alternative was favoured through the establishment of Garden Cities: 'there should be encouraged the starting of new industries and the removal of existing factories to garden cities which should be founded in the country where the inhabitants will live close to their work under the best possible conditions.'

This Report has great significance in the history of strategic land-use planning. It was the first Government Committee Report to advocate dispersal and decentralisation on a comprehensive scale. No doubt heavily influenced by the Garden City movement, it powerfully endorsed what became conventional orthodoxy twenty years later. The implied state role in securing population and industrial distribution was detailed in respect of London. A general plan for London's reconstruction was advocated, with a new authority covering an area wider than the existing LCC: 'a plan should be prepared now which should broadly assign to the various districts in and about London their respective functions in the future, so that every reconstruction scheme may conform to such a plan in its main details.'

The Final Report, of less consequence than the Interim Report, was submitted in April 1921. Once again the work was Chamberlain's. As he wrote to his sister Hilda, 'I had a very successful meeting of my Unhealthy Areas Committee on Wednesday; I spent a lot of time going through the report, re-drafting and adding to it, and the Committee simply opened its mouth and swallowed everything at a gulp.'

Many years were to elapse before the scale of city reconstruction plans which he was advocating, could come to fruition – and in the very different circumstances of a world war. But in 1926, as Minister of Health, he was able to move a little further along the road. Having received a LCC deputation to discuss the provision of playing fields in Greater London, he took the initiative in 1927, of calling a conference of the LCC and the surrounding County Councils and Boroughs to consider their collaboration on the preparation of a Greater London Regional Plan.

He addressed the Committee at its first meeting.[12] Making it clear that the Ministry's task in this venture was to encourage and assist, and in no way to do the work of the local authorities, he nonetheless offered some important suggestions. For example, he floated the idea of 'deliberately planned new towns, satellite towns, as the phrase sometimes goes, where you get sufficient concentration of population to conduce to effective government, to economy in services, and probably also to some reduction in the traffic problem.' He went on to say bluntly 'what I think we have to aim at is a decentralisation of our great city.' Garden cities represented a method of achieving this, perhaps 'by the appointment of some special commission, some body whose business it would be to take the initiative, to search for the necessary sites, and in some way to find the financial accommodation which would be necessary to give the thing a start.' (In fact, it was to take a long time for Government to move towards a national policy of population and employment distribution. A Departmental Committee on Garden Cities and Satellite Towns, chaired by Lord Marley, was appointed in 1931. It reported in 1934, advocating the fullest adoption of Garden City development – but no steps were taken to achieve this. In 1937, Chamberlain as Prime Minister, set up a Royal Commission on the Distribution of Industrial Population, under the chairmanship of Sir Montagu Barlow. The findings of this recommended control over the national development of land, but the Commission did not report until 1940, when the political situation was very different.

In his address of 1927, Chamberlain went on to speculate about a surrounding agricultural belt, which might accommodate parks and playing fields, although he recognised the cost of this. With regard to built-up areas he advocated zoning, the planned allocation of land for different uses: 'it is bound to come, and I do not think it can be very long delayed.' His long speech continued, touching on most aspects of the comprehensive planning task the Committee had before it.

It was a brave and instructive address, representing a positive town planning stance. Raymond Unwin, having recently retired, was appointed Technical Advisor. His Greater London Regional Planning Committee Reports of 1929 and 1933, put forward important principles for metropolitan planning, and his advocacy of a green girdle for Greater London led directly to the Green Belt (London and Home Counties) Act (1938).

While Chamberlain was carrying out his reforms at national level, there were two local authority politicians who were equally active in the field of reform. One was Herbert Morrison and the other E. D. Simon.

Morrison was Mayor of Hackney in 1920 and continued to serve on the Borough Council until 1925.[13] He became a member of the LCC in 1922 and as MP for Hackney South, he was Minister of Transport (1929–31). He quickly rose to the top in the London Labour Party and throughout the 1920s put forward lists of projects in Party policy statements. These included housing, town planning, slum clearance, the establishment of new towns or garden cities in the home counties, public improvement schemes and the transformation of neglected, private and public squares into public recreation grounds. He became Leader of the LCC in 1934 and for the remainder of that decade he applied his organising genius to the needs of the capital. He drew up programmes for housing, town planning, education, health and parks, and success-fully insitituted a town planning scheme over the whole of London. During the 1920s the Municipal Reformers (Conservatives) had re-jected the idea of preparing either a general plan for London, or Schemes to which building in particular areas would have to con-form. The Municipal Reformers' prevarication provoked outside bodies, notably the London Society, to try to seize the initiative in preparing a Plan for London. Labour's election victory of 1934, which brought Morrison to power, changed the situation. He ac-quired land on the South Bank for its development, and he was res-ponsible for the new Waterloo Bridge. Morrison ruled London and controlled his Labour Party with extraordinary efficiency. He had three of his closest party colleagues in his inner cabinet: Charles Latham (chairman of Finance Committee), Isaac Hayward (Chief Whip) and Lewis Silkin (Chairman of Housing Committee).

Of rather different outlook was E. D. (Sir Ernest) Simon, chair-man of Manchester's Housing Committee (1919–23) and Lord Mayor (1921–22). He was an industrialist and an active Liberal city politician, who wrote and lectured widely on planning and hous-ing matters. As a parliamentarian, he was Parliamentary Secretary to the Minister of Health in 1929. A great advocate of housing re-form, he successfully steered the city into the purchase of the Tat-ton Estate, covering more than 2500 acres to the south beyond the city boundary. He was also responsible for the implementation of Wythenshawe Garden Suburb, which was mooted in 1918 and be-gun in 1928 to the design of Barry Parker. The estate of ten re-sidential neighbourhoods was enclosed by an agricultural belt; at that time it was one of the largest areas of comprehensively planned development to be carried out by a single agency.

This example shows how local government might be regarded as a political laboratory where useful experiments can be later adopted as a basis for national legislation. The initiatives taken by some county councils in attempts to curb ribbon development are another example.[14] For a long time central Government did no-thing to prevent the tentacular outward spread of cities; but it was finally pushed into action by the efforts of a number of counties. In 1925, Middlesex CC promoted a Local Bill which included provi-sions for the council to acquire land up to 200 yards on either side of an arterial road. In 1931 Surrey CC followed suit, in 1933 Essex CC obtained similar powers and other councils prepared to follow. The Minister of Health took action. The King's Speech of Novem-ber 1934 announced that a Bill would be introduced 'if time permits, for the control of building development along the main thoroughfares.' The Restriction of Ribbon Development Act received the Royal Assent in August 1935.

For many local authorities, however, town planning remained a small part of their work during the 1920s and 1930s. This is not to say that some development projects did not proceed; bridges were built, such as those across the Tyne at Newcastle and the Aire at Boothferry; tunnels were constructed as under the Mersey at Liverpool; bypasses and new roads were laid out. Four million dwellings were built between the wars, one quarter on local authority estates. By the end of the 1930s one dwelling in three had been built since 1918; the suburban spread was now in earnest. In the old parts of cities a start had been made on slum clearance. New industrial development took place, and Slough was an early example of the popular trading estate. Towards the end of the 1930s, sites for aerodromes were being found. The urban map of England was extending: between 1927 and 1939 it has been estimated that 2 per cent of the land surface changed from rural to urban.

It cannot be pretended that town planning legislation made much difference to what occurred. Only 5 per cent of the land of England was subject to operative town planning Schemes at the outbreak of war (although 73 per cent had become subject to interim development control). Right-wing commitment to the sanctity of property had emasculated legislation with regard to compensation and betterment; it remained a fact that local authorities had great difficulty in refusing permission to develop because the compensation payable would be beyond their resources. Furthermore, the fear of giving too much power to the State, both local and central, meant that development took place through the largely unfettered operation of the private market rather than the guidance of the public sector. The history of town planning legislation suggests that most was gained at times of threatened danger to national safety (the German threat before 1914 and bolshevism after 1918), social instability and industrial unrest. Above all, progress was made in the emotion of post-war reconstruction, though that determination soon evaporated. In these circumstances the preparation of long-term plans for whole cities, and the strategic guidance of population and employment distribution (as for Greater London) both now recognised as key elements in town planning practice, received little official political support. The constancy of political will, required by town planning, did not exist.

This meant also that related elements of town planning, which required a commitment to Government intervention in or influence over private rights, failed to develop. Regional economic planning which called for strategic land–use location policies was stillborn; the Government was hesitant enough in interfering in economic matters alone, never mind attempting to coordinate these with land use and other policies. It was a similar situation with National Parks. Addison's National Park Committee had reported in 1931; they saw a need for adequate measures for preserving the countryside and found favour in National Parks as an element in a nation-wide scheme of other open spaces. They thought that a National Authority would be necessary to supplement the effort of local authorities. Nothing was done, and it was left to a Private Member's Bill to attempt to secure access agreements on private land in rambling and hiking areas; in the event the Access to Mountains Act (1939) was an abortive measure.[15]

Thus the Town Planning Acts between the wars were of small significance. They did, however, provide a statutory framework for local authority action, and in the best cases there is no doubt that improved environments resulted in the form of coordinated development and higher design and layout standards. Regional advisory committees flourished in attempts to coordinate action amongst a large number of authorities, but there was no cutting edge. In the meantime consultants prepared commissioned plans and their proven professional capacity pointed the way forward. Sometimes Private Acts secured town planning objectives. However, the political scene was changing and new attitudes were being formed. A very different stage in town planning history was about to begin.

Chapter three

DEVELOPMENTS IN TOWN PLANNING – WAR TIME
AND POST WAR

THE MOOD OF THE NATION

By the mid 1930s, there was a growing sense of disillusionment at the state of Britain. That sense of shame and disappointment fed a resolve to tackle the many economic, social and environmental problems of both urban and rural areas, although the methods to be adopted were for some time obscure and uncertain. However, the experience of war introduced a new, vital ingredient, and within a remarkably short time, plans for reconstruction provided the context for town planning in the 1940s.

This is not the place to deal at length with the social and economic problems of inter-war Britain, but we must acknowledge their importance. They greatly contributed to a new mood in the country: a determination to replace and rebuild. This proved to be highly conducive to town planning as a contribution to a future Britain. A poverty of housing and environmental conditions was the target for many contemporary observers. George Orwell's *The Road to Wigan Pier* (1937) protested at the ugliness of northern towns: 'As you walk through the industrial towns you lose yourself in labyrinths of little brick houses blackened by smoke, festering in planless chaos round miry alleys and little cindered yards where there are stinking dust-bins and lines of grimy washing and half ruinous WCs.' The lunar landscape of Wigan and the sulphur smelling environment of Sheffield were obscenities before a nation. J. B. Priestley's *English Journey* (1934) had earlier communicated a similar sense of outrage at so much squalor in the midst of plenty. A bus ride from Coventry brought him to Birmingham: '. . . we were passing houses and shops and factories. Did all this look like the entrance into the second city in England? It did. It looked a dirty muddle.'

Urban poverty was also high on the agenda of social enquiry. Studies in provincial towns suggested that one quarter of working–class children were being born into families that could not afford the minimum diet specified by the British Medical Association. This partly explains the health campaign of the 1930s and puts into context the Physical Training and Recreation Act of 1937. George Orwell's *Keep the Aspidistra Flying* (1936) described some to the features of the life led by those in penury: the penny-pinching existence marked by drab lodgings, hunger and an abiding sense of hopelessness made all the more acute by surroundings of privilege and plenty for others.

Some of the worst of the urban conditions, however, were disappearing. Overcrowding for example, with 14 per cent of the population of Great Britain living at more than two persons per room in 1921, had halved by 1939. Moreover, as a result of the anti-slum campaign, out of the 472,000 slum dwellings scheduled for closure in England and Wales, 272,000 had been dealt with by March 1939. Quarry Hill flats in Leeds, a project pioneered by the Rev. Charles Jenkinson, the local Labour Leader was a spectacular illustration of redevelopment. But on the other hand, Manchester could still report that one third of its total dwellings were unfit at the outbreak of war. Furthermore, in the rural areas housing standards remained depressed. In 1938 less than 30,000 agricultural holdings out of a total of 366,000 were served with electricity; just one holding in seven had piped water.

There was disappointment not only with the lack of progress but also with what had been achieved. Becontree, the east London estate developed in the 1920s, and Wythenshawe, the garden suburb for Manchester, may have been remarkable for their size; suburban developments throughout the country may have offered new forms of low density living. But the spread-out city raised difficulties, such as the length and cost of travel to work, and the sterility of social life was apparent. 'Come friendly bombs and fall on Slough' wrote Betjeman in his satirical poem 'Slough' (1938).

Failure to achieve very much in the countryside (for example, in help to agriculture or support for isolated rural communities) was made worse by the inability to stop the excesses of building sprawl. There was a sustained outflow of labour and population from the land as the wages of the agricultural worker remained markedly lower (and his hours longer) than those of the unskilled industrial labourer. Meanwhile the countryside was subject to despoilation by sporadic building development, a consequence of the absence of adequate planning safeguards. The creation of a new pressure group, the Council for the Preservation of Rural England in 1926, the launching of the magazine *The Countryman* in 1927, and Clough Williams-Ellis' book, *Britain and the Octopus* (1928), (in which the tentacles of Britain's spreading cities were pictured as undesirable encroachment), all illustrate growing concern. Meanwhile the countryside was increasingly the place for mass recreation; these were the years of the rambling and hiking cults. The great attractions were the grouse moors of the north, in private ownership for their sporting rights. The inevitable conflict of interest had the flashpoint of trespass, and mass civil disobedience in the form of deliberate trespass formed the background to the Access to Mountains Act (1939) and the wider National Parks movement.

Anger and bitterness also resulted from unemployment. The structural decline of the older industrial areas based on coal, textiles, heavy engineering and shipbuilding, compounded by the loss of world markets during the the First World War and the world economic recession, produced a new set of social and economic questions for Britain. Unemployment hit new areas (the disadvantaged regions rather than London) with a severity not experienced before. National unemployment reached 9 per cent in 1924, and did not fall below that for many years. In 1930 it was 20 per cent; in 1933 three million were unemployed, 23 per cent of the insured workforce. There were chronic concentrations, particularly on Tyneside (Jarrow) and South Wales (Merthyr Tydfil), where unemployment was long term. Social distress was acute; unemployment was essentially male, social security was limited, and there was little by way of an 'informal economy' (as in the countryside or in odd-jobbing) on which households could fall back.

Political attitudes were considerably affected. The second volume of Beveridge's *Unemployment* (1930), and J. M. Keynes' *The General Theory of Employment Interest and Money* (1936) provided both explanation and prescription. Ellen Wilkinson's *The Town that was Murdered* (1939), told the story of Jarrow. A pronounced regional drift of population had become apparent, and the contrast between a deprived and a relatively privileged Britain assumed a sharp geographical focus. London and the home counties were the magnet of attraction; the population of Greater London increased by 2 million between the wars, 1¼ million of which came from migration. In 1934, when Jarrow's unemployment rate was 68 per cent, that for Coventry and Oxford was 5 per cent and High Wycombe 3.3 per cent.

An interest developed in planning as a form of central direction in national affairs. The next chapter will show how the creation of Political and Economic Planning (PEP) in 1931 and the political writings of Harold Macmillan were illustrations of this. A concern for how the land of Britain was used (or misused) was reflected in the setting up of the Land Utilisation Survey in 1930. The right use of land, this time not just in terms of suburban housing but on a national scale, was held to be important; the promise of land-use planning, which gave control over particular uses and broad locations, encouraged town planning to adopt a strategic remit.

By the end of the 1930s there was thus a widespread intolerance of the circumstances which had produced the conditions, not only of the inter-war period but also those inherited from the nineteenth century. When the time came, a determination to rebuild fed on this deeply-rooted sentiment. Other countries seemed to be putting their houses in order: Hitler, Mussolini and Stalin had their methods. However, whatever the attractions of central direction (through National Socialism or Communism), Britain chose the parliamentary way, building on the institutions we had come to regard with favour. Winifred Holtby's *South Riding* (1936), interestingly subtitled 'an English landscape' centred around the workings of local government, and showed the resolve to retain the British way of things. There was an inner quality in British life which was worth rediscovering, if only the means could be found. As Jan Struther's *Mrs Miniver* (1939) pointed out:

But it oughtn't to need a war to make a nation paint its kerbstones white, carry rear-lamps on its bicycles, and give all its slum children a holiday in the country. And it oughtn't to need a war to make us talk to each other in buses, and invent our own amusements in the evenings, and live simply, and eat sparingly, and recover the use of our legs, and get up early enough to see the sun rise. However, it has needed one: which is about the severest criticism our civilisation could have.

So the mood for reconstruction was set. There was no doubting that while the inter-war years had seen progress, not enough had been achieved. Rowntree's second social survey of York (1935) was a convincing illustration.[1] (The first survey had been carried out in 1899.) Standards had risen appreciably. In 1899, scarcely a working-class house in York had either a bath or a garden; in 1936 25 per cent had both. Rowntree summarised the improvements:

The economic condition of the workers is better by 30 per cent than in 1899, though working hours are shorter. Housing is immeasurably better, health is better, education is better. Cheap means of transport, the provision of public libraries and cheap books, the wireless, the cinema and other places of entertainment, have placed within reach of everyone forms of recreation unknown, and some of them unthought of, forty years ago.

All standards are relative, however, and from the point of view of housing Rowntree concluded that while 30 per cent of the workers were well housed, and 40 per cent lived under conditions short of the ideal but nevertheless not detrimental to health, the remaining 30 per cent lived under conditions 'unsatisfactory from every standpoint'. Poverty and the economic system that underpinned it remained the key issue:

Great though the progress made during the last forty years has been, there is no cause for satisfaction in the fact that in a country so rich as England, over 30 per cent of the workers in a typically provincial city should have incomes so small that it is beyond their means to live even at the stringently economic level adopted as a minimum in this survey, nor in the fact that almost half the children of working class parents spend the first five years of their lives in poverty and that almost a third of them live below the poverty line for ten years or more.

No national social survey of Great Britain existed, though a reasonable picture could be pieced together from a number of local surveys. A national report on overcrowding in England and Wales had highlighted London and the North East as problem areas. The Social Surveys of Merseyside, Sheffield, Bristol and Southampton revealed that between 12 and 15 per cent of their families and between 22 and 30 per cent of their children were living below the poverty line. Sir John Orr calculated in 1936 that one-tenth of the nation's population, including nearly one-quarter of its children, had a diet lacking in all the constituents most essential to health. And in 1939 and 1940, evacuation from London and the big cities revealed to an unsuspecting wider population the personal conditions and habits of degraded urban dwellers.

In 1939, Margaret Bondfield, a former Minister of Labour (1929–31), chaired a small group of working professional women to review the urban conditions which might be held responsible for the conditions of the evacuees. Their report (1943)[2] held up a mirror of urban Britain and put forward a hope for the future based on education, health, social and housing reform. Bondfield's Preface expressed the spirit of war-time Britain:

This book will be, I hope, the last of its kind. It exposes a weakness which runs through a great deal of the effort to reform certain bad conditions of living. We are too easily satisfied with the top crust of results. A housing crusade secures a scheme of slum clearance and lo! a bright patch of town planning to which we bring enquiring visitors. We accept their congratulations and too often our crusading zeal ends at that point. But it is patchwork reform, and so often the pieces do not fit.

This was the pressure for reform, this determination to get things right which captured an intense political mood. It provided the key for a decade; indeed it was so powerful that it lasted for another quarter of a century. What class and sectional interests had failed to deliver, the 'national interest' serving the needs of the whole community must now be given a chance. *When We Build Again* (1941) was a study of Birmingham by the Bournville Village Trust, but it was a title which typified its period for a whole nation. The politics of war-time and post-war town planning were grounded in this context. There could be no clearer illustration of how town planning is shaped by social values, attitudes and aspirations.

THE WAR TIME YEARS

With the war, a new political situation prevailed. The advent of war released the psychological floodgates for reconstruction (social, moral and physical), demanding new machinery of government and ultimately new legislation. The next four years were to be very eventful. Cullingworth has mapped out this complicated period in his Offical History of war-time environmental planning.[3] Reconstruction machinery originated with the Cabinet's War Aims Committee, set up in August 1940. It had been given a small secretariat, and taken over by Arthur Greenwood, who was appointed Minister without Portfolio in December. In February 1941, a Cabinet Committee on Reconstruction Problems was created under Greenwood's chairmanship. By October it had been supplanted by a smaller and more workable committee of half a dozen members; it was still chaired by Greenwood.

In the meantime, the old Office of Works had become (in September 1940) the Ministry of Works and Buildings. Sir John (later Lord) Reith, former Governor of the BBC and Chairman of Imperial Airways, and during 1940 successively Minister of Information and Minister of Transport was invited to become the first Minister of this Department. He staked a claim for responsibility for planning and reconstruction arising out of the war and the post-war period. This created difficulties for the Ministry of Health and functions had to be divided: Health retained the statutory town and country planning function while Reith was to plan for the future through a Reconstruction Group in his Department. After a long delay the Department's title was changed in February 1942 and Reith became Minister of Works and Planning. Within a fortnight, however, he was asked to resign and he was replaced by Lord Portal.

Stuart (editor of the Reith Diaries) maintains that Reith was ineffective.[4] First he had a distaste for Churchill and his close associates, including Greenwood. Second he had a difficult manner:

his dedicated determination to keep post war problems in the forefront of the minds of his colleagues. This was precient, even statesmanlike . . . but it was wholly unrealistic. To expect plans for a national transport system to be seriously considered at the height of the Battle of Britain was naively innocent; and to seek Cabinet priority for the consideration of general post war planning when the British Empire in the Far East was in the process of collapse was little closer to reality. On the other hand his enthusiasm and sense of vision was captivating. Reith's advice to a delegation from blitzed Coventry was typical: 'I told them that if I were in their position I would plan boldly and comprehensively, and that I would not at this stage worry about finance or local boundaries. They had not expected such advice . . . But it was what they wanted and needed; it put new heart into them.'[5]

Reith's place in these confusing early war-time years was established, by his appointment of the Expert Committee on Compensation and Betterment, chaired by Mr Justice Uthwatt (January 1941), and of the Committee on Land Utilisation in Rural Areas, chaired by Lord Justice Scott (October 1941). Uthwatt reported in September 1942 (Cmd 6386) and Scott a month earlier (Cmd 6378). These two Reports complement the Barlow Report on the Distribution of the Industrial Population (Cmd 6153), (1940), and this trilogy provided the working references for post-war planning.

To meet the national problems of industrial location, Barlow recommended a Central Authority. But a Minority Report by Professor Patrick Abercrombie and two other Commissioners felt that this proposal had not been carried to its logical conclusion, and they recommended that far-reaching powers be given to a new Government Department. Uthwatt in his Report worked on the assumption that a Central Planning Authority would be set up. Scott also assumed the establishment of such an Authority. But it was not as easy as that. As Cullingworth remarks, 'the simplistic notion of a central planning Authority with wide (if not omnipotent) powers over other government departments rapidly foundered. Indeed, it is unlikely that it would have proceeded as far as it did had it not

been for the preoccupation of senior ministers with urgent war affairs, the incredibly diffuse nature of reconstruction planning, and
the singlemindedness of Reith.'[6] In the event, innovation was limited first to the transfer of town and country planning functions
in June 1942, to the Ministry of Works and Planning, and later to
the setting up of a Ministry of Town and Country Planning in
February 1943. It was the intention that this new Ministry would
be assigned a positive role in central planning.

During 1943 and 1944, Committees and Cabinet wrestled with
the recommendations of the Uthwatt Report for a Town and Country Planning Bill. The problems centred on the level of compensation to be paid for land and property acquired by local authorities,
and the procedure to be followed. This had to be speedy enough to
get development going in the first place, but it was necessary that
owners should be informed and allowed to object, if they chose.
Political battle lines were drawn. The Earl of Selbourne, Minister
of Economic Warfare, summarised the issue:

It must necessarily sometimes be difficult for Conservatives, Liberals and
Socialists to agree about post war legislation. In Town and Country Planning the Socialist and the Liberal will wish to extend State interference
with private trade and property much further than most of the Conservatives will think necessary or desirable. Many Conservatives hold that State
planning can easily be carried to a point where it will impede development
and impair freedom, without improving anything. For the sake of avoiding
controversy that might delay measures of reconstruction desired by everyone, I would make many concessions to my socialist colleagues, and do not
contest the unprecedented powers of land acquisition embodied in the
Bill. No compromise, however, appears to be legitimate on the question of
fair compensation to persons dispossessed of their property.[7]

The Bill had a difficult passage. A principle was established that
compensation would be payable at 1939 prices; the result was that
the Conservatives objected that landowners would get no more than
the 1939 prices, but Labour, the LCC and some local authorities
objected because it would prevent them paying landowners less
than the 1939 prices. The fact was that the big property organisations regarded Uthwatt as concealed nationalisation; Lord Brocket
of the Property Owners' Protection Society denounced it as unpro-
voked aggression. Michael Foot has hinted at the great tussle behind the scenes, quoting Lewis Silkin who called the Bill a 'miser-
able and mean measure which represents a victory by the land owning interests over the public interest. If the Labour Party accepts it,
even in principle, it will be guilty of having betrayed the hopes of

all who have placed their trust in our movement... It will have passed a sentence of death upon comprehensive planning for many generations to come.'[8]

Labour abstained on the Second Reading of the Bill, while seeking to improve the measure drastically at Committee stage. Churchill himself intervened, and a committee under Attlee's chairmanship worked out an acceptable compromise. The general principle that compensation should be assessed by references to prices current at March 1939 was adhered to, but all owner occupiers were to be given the right to a supplementary payment, determined according to the circumstances of each particular case. The additional payment was limited to 30 per cent of the 1939 value of the property. There was still Conservative opposition to the exclusion of investors from the more generous compensation provisions, but the Bill went through and received the Royal Assent in November 1944. But as Foot concludes, 'the intricacies of parliamentary manoevre over the Town and Country Planning Bill cast a gleam of light across the whole field of British politics. The question of the ownership of land was the real rock on which the coalition was broken. Here was where property stood its ground against prevailing sentiment of the age and political accommodations were forbidden.'[9]

During the early 1940s, remarkable changes took place in political acceptance of town planning. The war-time coalition Government was obliged to present a united front to Parliament and the public; and while the issues of reconstruction were huge and complex, a world war was being fought. There was a readiness by many Ministers, to be pragmatic rather than doctrinaire and to leave considerable initiative to officials. But despite this, Ministers jealously looked after the interests of their own Departments, and the birth and subsequent life of the Ministry of Town and Country Planning itself was not without antagonisms.

There was however, one office which retained a degree of independence. This was the Scottish Office, and Thomas Johnston, Secretary of State in these years, has described the ways in which he kept one step in front of his Whitehall colleages:

Every now and again some ingenious gentleman in London would exude a plan for a centralised planning of our industries, our housing, our roads, rails, canals, airports, our shops, our churches – yes, the location of our churches! – and our beer shops. And you never knew in what rapturous moment some persuasive hierarchy at a ministry might have been authorised to so plan and blueprint us. Before any such dark night fell, and to

41

ward off the menace, it was essential that we had in Scotland a fait accompli, a regional association of local authorities in the East and one in the West, each appointing at Government expense a distinguished planning consultant, and authorising major outline plans into which all the plans of the governing bodies in the area could be dovetailed. In the spring of 1943 we got three regional planning bodies set agoing with Sir Patrick Abercrombie as consultant in the West and Sir Frank Mears in the East, and thereafter, when centralised planning boiled up in London, I could always point to the prior existence of my regional associations and say that centralisation must stop south of the Cheviots.[10]

The mood in 1945 was buoyant and confident. Planning had won the war, so why could it not win the peace? Town planning promised control over land use, coordination of physical development, the reconstruction of cities and protection of the countryside with a revivified agriculture. State direction, both local and central, was the way forward; private interests in land and development had to be subservient to the public interest. Sir Ernest Simon summarised these arguments in 1945:

Britain has shown what a democracy can do in war time. We have doubled our output; we have abolished unemployment; we have organised ourselves magnificently for war purposes . . . If we can tackle the problems of peace with anything like the same sense of purpose, the same devotion, and the same efficiency as we have shown during the war, the Rebuilding of Britain will be child's play. . . . if we decide that we do mean to rebuild Britain in twenty years, then my analysis shows conclusively that we can only succeed if we tackle this great task on the same broad lines as those which are winning the war: the planning must be done by the Government and local authorities, the decision as to what is to be built and how and when and where must be made by the Government. . . .[11]

The confidence behind these remarks may be intepreted as misplaced naivety. Nevertheless, it was a confidence widely shared, born of a sustained idealism, a commitment to the housing and environmental reform of earlier decades and a determination to grasp the nettle once and for all. Simon was 'confident that we can in twenty years rebuild Britain, so as to enable every inhabitant, child or adult, to live in a healthy home, in a neighbourhood so planned as to allow easy access for all the members of the family to their places of work and recreation. This is one of the great reforms which is entirely in our own hands; international affairs (apart from war) cannot interfere with it'.

SILKIN'S BILLS

Lewis Silkin became Minister of Town and Country Planning as the new Labour Government swept into power in 1945 with a landslide victory (Labour 393, Conservatives 213, Liberals 12, ILP 3, Communists 2, Independents 14). The next five years were a period of vigorous reforming legislation. Town planning was considerably boosted and three Acts in 1946, 1947 and 1949 laid the basis for the post-war system.

The location of industry was a matter for the Board of Trade, but the Distribution of Industry Act (1945) was rushed through Parliament before the Dissolution, suffering some emasculation in the process but nonetheless establishing the foundation of British regional policy until 1960. The pre-war Special Areas were redefined and renamed Development Areas. Factory building and provision of infrastructure was to be aided, and there was to be control over new building through the granting of Industrial Development Certificates. There was by this time widespread agreement on this aspect of a planned economy, largely due to the satisfactory experience of the war years. Hugh Dalton, President of the Board of Trade during the second half of the war, has recorded his good relations with leading industrialists on matters of location policy.[12]

Abercrombie's *Greater London Plan* (1944) proposed a redistribution of London's population on a massive scale; more than a million people were to move, including 380,000 to eight or ten new satellite towns beyond the green belt. W. S. Morrison, Minister of Town and Country Planning, communicated his view to Lord Woolton, Minister of Reconstruction, that Stevenage seemed well suited for a first experiment. On taking office in August 1945 Silkin was equally attracted to the idea, and although nothing had been said in the Labour Party manifesto before the election, within nine months the Government had introduced a New Towns Bill.

To help his case, Silkin, jointly with the Secretary of State for Scotland, appointed a departmental committee in October, to consider the general question of new towns and how they should be established. Lord Reith was appointed chairman. An interim report was hurried through because Silkin wanted to make progress with Stevenage. A second interim report and a final report were presented by July 1946. (Cmds 6759, 6794 and 6876.)

The New Towns Bill (April 1946) provided for the designation of sites for New Towns, the setting up of Development Corporations for their development and the range of powers they would use. The Bill had an unopposed second reading, the only objection coming from Lord Hinchingbrooke, who denounced the Bill as 'frankly totalitarian in form'. In Standing Committee, only one amendment, to give protection to the requirements of food production, was pressed to a division, but was rejected. The Bill had an unopposed third reading but it was once more condemned by Hinchingbrooke as 'a State experiment in the life and happiness of our people and in my opinion like all State experiments, it will work havoc, bitterness and grave social damage.'[13] It received the Royal Assent in December.

A much more complicated measure was the Town and Country Planning Bill. This had a long pedigree, originating as a Bill to deal with the Uthwatt recommendations, but ending as a composite measure, tackling the problems of compensation and betterment and providing the basis of statutory land use planning dependent on the Development Plan and a system of development control. The financial provisions were radical and gave rise to considerable political controversy. Where land was developed, the increase in its value resulting from the granting of planning permission was secured for the community by imposing a development charge, to be assessed and collected by a Central Land Board. This was recoupment of betterment, and the levy was 100 per cent. For compensation, a sum of £300 million was set aside from which payments were to be made to land owners in respect of property depreciated by restrictions imposed by the Act. Since 1909, town planning legislation had sought to tackle the compensation and betterment problem; the 1947 Act in effect nationalised development value, and this meant that a person who was refused permission to develop land was not normally entitled to compensation.

The Bill was inherently complex, and over 1400 amendments were tabled, in roughly equal proportions by Government and Opposition. Cullingworth summarises the opposition view:

the Bill made great changes in the powers of local authorities before time was given to them and other affected bodies to study its provisions; it fixed an arbitrary sum for compensation which did not purport to be just and was not determined by independent inquiry: it laid down no principles for the allocation of this sum; it gave insufficient indication of the principles to be followed in levying development charges; it continued to employ the now invalid 1939 standard to compensate for land compulsorily acquired; it made possible discrimination against proper development by private persons; and it would create uncertainty (thus hampering and delaying development by leaving for subsequent orders matters requiring definition in the Bill).[14]

In spite of these views, the party differences were relatively mild, particularly compared with the extremism and the campaigning by special interests that marked the Acts of 1932 and 1944.

Government gave way on one issue only, the 1939 standard. The 30 per cent supplement for owner occupiers, introduced in order to get agreement for the 1944 Bill, was increased to 60 per cent. After further reconsideration the 1939 standard was abolished and the new basis became current market value. The Bill received the Royal Assent in August 1947.

Silkin's third town planning measure concerned National Parks.[15] Once again, the matter was of long standing, and as with New Towns the Bill received little opposition. During the war years, a vigorous lobby had exercised considerable pressure for National Parks to be set up after the war as part of the nation's reconstruction programme. From 1942 onwards, John Dower was surveying possible National Park areas for the Ministry of Works and Planning. His work developed into a comprehensive study and was published in May 1945 as a personal report to the Minister of Town and Country Planning. W. S. Morrison presented Dower's Report to the War Cabinet Reconstruction Committee and accompanying it was another Memorandum by the Secretary of State for Scotland with a report from the Scottish National Parks Survey Committee. This had been working concurrently with Dower. The Minister sought permission to set up a Preparatory National Parks Commission, but this was denied, pending further consideration. Morrison proceeded to set up a committee, chaired by Sir Arthur Hobhouse to consider further the Dower Report.

In August 1945, Silkin was the new Minister, and as with New Towns, he was enthusiastic about National Parks. Hobhouse reported in 1947 and his Bill was introduced in March 1949. Silkin found that the main opposition came from his own colleagues and officials, rather than from the politicians of other parties. The Ministry's officials had no great interest in National Parks, or the idea of a National Parks Commission, and the Treasury persistently objected. Moreover, there were disagreements over whether the Parks should be under national or local control. When the Bill was going through the House, Silkin was pressed for assurances on Park Planning Committees and the proportion of nominated members. But despite this, the Bill had a fairly easy passage and the political teeth of the land owners, who had feared trespass, wholesale land acquisition and disruption to farming, were drawn. The emotive battles of the Access to Mountains Bill (1939) were a long decade ago, and the Bill was passed in December 1949. It was assumed that Scottish legislation would follow the next year, but it did not, and as delay continued, the argument that the Scottish situation was different from that of England grew stronger. A change of Government in 1951 held no new prospects and in 1952 Lord Home, Minister of State, pleaded difficulties of finance and a congested legislative programme.

Silkin's seat was abolished in a Parliamentary Boundary Review and after the General Election of 1950 he went to the Lords. He could look back on his five years with considerable satisfaction. Without a seat in the Cabinet he had convinced his colleagues and piloted three major Bills through the House, one of inordinate complexity. All three were to stand the test of time, providing important planks for post-war town planning. He had a virtually new Department and he had to protect and enhance its status. At a time of a muted political opposition, his battles were internal. The Treasury, in particular, viewed his Department with anxiety, and his officials were concerned about their collective status. Such was the context of his legislative programme.

POST-WAR TOWN PLANNING

By the end of the 1940s, the country's political mood had altered and the impetus for further social change was lost. Political programmes were no longer fired by promises of post-war reconstruction; indeed, the delays and restrictions associated in the public mind with planning made such promises unwelcome. The general election of February 1950 returned Attlee to power but the Labour majority over Conservative was now just eighteen, and the Liberals had nine seats. Labour was running out of steam, riven by internal quarrels in the cabinets, and in the election of September 1951, in which Attlee hoped to increase his majority and bring his colleagues to heel, the Conservatives were returned with 321 seats to Labour's 295; the Liberals had just six. Political commentators said that the country wanted a period of consolidation and a lifting of the burden of wartime controls.

Thirteen years of Conservative administration resulted in less constriction and, perhaps rather unexpectedly, significant bursts of economic growth. A downturn in the early 1960s allowed Labour to return in 1964 on a knife-edge overall majority of four, on a programme of a long-term, planned boom. In 1966 their overall majority was increased to a healthy 97. 1970–4 saw the Conservatives in office, 1974–9 Labour (although a minority Government throughout), and in 1979 the Conservatives were returned again on a programme of freedom, individual initiative and restrictions on the growth of the State.

The thirty years since 1950 form a distinct period, not only in British politics (three decades of single party governments), but also in social experiences, yet it is by no means homogeneous. Each decade has its own characteristics, but there are some which are common to each. The broad directions of the welfare state laid down in the 1940s have continued through a combination of State centralism and an extension of local authority services. Similarly the broad outlines of the town planning system have been maintained. But the idealism which nourished it, and the demands of post-war reconstruction which shaped it, soon lost their fervour, their certainty and conviction. Shibboleths of town planning ideology did not remain inviolable for long. Even the widely–respected assertion of the need to decentralise our big cities was soon challenged: the sociologists Willmott and Young looked at the experiences of planned redevelopment in East London and concluded that it was harmful to the communities it was intended to serve.[16]

The achievement of a promised future, by ensuring the right use of land, seemed an inordinately protracted affair, and there were queries as to whether the cost was justified. The statutory planning system of Development Plan preparation and the day to day control of development, according to the provisions of the Plan, tended to lapse into dull, regulatory, local authority bureaucracy. What had been promised as bold and imaginative turned out to be sterile and couched in terms of professional mumbo-jumbo. Few could understand the multiplicity of issues which a comprehensive system of town planning entailed. In retrospect it seems bizarre that in 1968, twenty years after the operative date of the 1947 Act, it was necessary to bring in new legislation to abolish the inflexibility of the existing system. The 1947 Act was itself intended to replace the inflexibility of the pre-war system. Town planning lost its edge, it seemed not to deliver. In many ways the life of a Cabinet Minister became not the crusade for reform that Silkin must have enjoyed, but a sparring match between politician and civil servant, a series of attempts by one to control the other. In 1964 Crossman observed:

My Minister's room is like a padded cell, and in certain ways I am like a person who is suddenly certified a lunatic and put safely into this great, vast room, cut off from real life and surrounded by male and female trained nurses and attendants. When I am in a good mood they occasionally allow an ordinary human being to come and visit me; but they make sure that I behave right, and that the other person behaves right; and they know how to handle me.[17]

The postwar planning machine has been broadly maintained (and supported by all shades of political opinion). There is however, one exception, relating to the financial provisions of the 1947 Act. The question of compensation and betterment touches raw political nerves, and deep rooted biases and prejudices have made town planning, in relation to land and property, something of a political football. The broad outlines of the story are discussed in planning textbooks, but these tend to omit the political cut and thrust behind the scenes.[18]

The 1947 provisions did not work smoothly, and perhaps the 100 per cent charge was the biggest single difficulty. There was vigorous political objection. R. R. Costain addressing the Association of London Property Owners in February 1947, maintained that the scheme would 'stop everyone but the most wealthy builders from ever building again' and argued that it was as if the Minister of Health (in charge of housing) had turned to the Minister of Town and Country Planning, saying 'I cannot stop private building, you stop it.' The Chairman of the Eastbourne Building and Planning Committee even resigned his post on the grounds that he could not be a party to the administration of the Town and Country Planning Act (1947) because the scheme was 'grossly unfair . . . legalised robbery' and 'nothing but communism'.[19]

The Conservative Government of 1951, committed to raising the level of construction activity, and particularly the rate of private house building, abolished development charges, though imposed a limit to the liability to compensation for planning restrictions. Betterment was to be collected through the blunt instrument of general taxation. But the system (via legislation in 1953 and 1954) created two values for land, according to whether it was sold in the open market or acquired by a public authority. Further legislation in 1959 restored fair market price as the basis of compensation for compulsory acquisition, and the result proved extremely costly to public authorities. Eight years later the system was changed again by Labour through the introduction of a capital gains tax, a new betterment levy and the establishment of the Land Commission.

The principle was that the capital gains tax was charged on increases in the current use value of land, while betterment levy was charged on increases in development value. The Land Commission, established with powers to buy land by agreement or compulsorily, in order to promote the development of land in a positive fashion, was abolished by the Conservatives in 1971, just as its predecessor, the Central Land Board had been abolished. Labour attempted again to tackle the problem a few years later, through John Silkin's Community Land Act of 1975 (the son following his father in dealing with the same problem thirty years later). This gave local authorities wider powers to acquire land for development, to hold it in the form of land banks, and to recoup the increase in value of land through a Development Land Tax. The Conservatives repealed this legislation in 1979, and the result is a complicated and sorry story reflecting British party political incompatibility with regard to land and property. Town planning's political context is nowhere better illustrated than in this failure to come to terms with the recoupment of development value and effective land management through State holdings of land.

Apart from this factor, however, the essential components of the post-war planning system remain the same; on occasions they have been equally strongly supported by Labour and Conservative Ministers, though perhaps for different reasons. We may offer the New Town policy as a classic illustration. By the time of the election in February 1950, Lewis Silkin and successive Secretaries of State for Scotland (Westwood and Woodburn) had established eight New Towns for London, two in Durham, one in the Midlands (Corby), one in South Wales and two in Scotland. Silkin's proposals in particular had met with no great enthusiasm from his ministerial colleagues, and a policy review was conducted when Dalton became Minister of Local Government and Planning (as the MTCP was now called). The basis of a new approach favoured 'town development' by local authorities, and in November 1951, when Macmillan became Minister of Housing and Local Government (the Department's name having changed again), the same intentions were adopted. The new Conservative Government pinned their hope on the machinery of the Town Development Act (1952), rather than on the New Towns. Indeed, New Towns came under increasing pressure, and for two and a half years Macmillan fended off opposition from at least two quarters: one from the Treasury which pleaded the need for economies and one from the Board of Trade which saw a conflict with its distribution of industry policy.

Cumbernauld was the only New Town designated in the 1950s, but early in the 1960s, political sympathies changed and once more they gained favour. Town development was not working all that well, county borough/county conflicts on overspill were difficult to resolve, and with revised population forecasts, New Towns were restored to priority. At one end of the political spectrum Sir Keith Joseph was an enthusiastic advocate, and at the other, Labour continued to designate New Towns. A further revision of population forecasts brought New Towns to an end, with the designation of Stonehouse in 1973. Town development also ceased. A new set of priorities now favours the development and restoration of the older, inner areas of cities; this policy was introduced by Labour and has been continued by the Conservatives.

Thus a period of twenty years saw considerable change so far as political commitment and Ministerial attitudes were concerned. Cullingworth refers to 'Silkin's deep personal involvement in establishing the first new towns, Macmillan's adroit manoeuvres to safeguard them, and Joseph's increasingly pragmatic commitment to them as effective instruments for implementing regional policy.'[20] Silkin certainly laid a firm foundation, but what followed was pragmatism rather than conviction. The New Towns were protected and promoted for a range of practical reasons; not least they were a convenient instrument for implementing a variety of policies.

The continuance of policy through pragmatism rather than by conviction might well summarise post-war town planning as a whole. New policies and new instruments for implementing them were forged in the heady years of 1946–50. They have been maintained, adapted and added to in the pursuit of changing objectives. The National Parks Commission has been replaced by the Countryside Commission, Structure Plans have replaced Development Plans, and Regional Strategies have replaced Regional Plans. Local authorities have become heavily involved in redevelopment both for housing and commercial purposes; with new road building they have transformed the inner areas of cities and their shopping and office centres. Throughout all this, the development control powers have ensured continuous management of development. But after the phases of plan making, commitment to overriding policy seems rare; perhaps only the green belt and restrictions on building in the countryside remain. Policies launched in the later 1940s have become strangely a political; they have attracted support from successive Ministers, and this has ensured their continuation. There is no longer a coherent, understood target for town planning which is put forward by one or other political party; the objectives are more diverse and fluid. Urban and regional management is now much less exciting than the town planning of the 1940s. The real political argument has descended to the local authorities and the political problems and conflicts in town planning are now at this level. It is the local politician who has to cope with mistakes of earlier decades. Nicholas Taylor, for example, the chairman of a London Borough Planning Committee, came to reflect on popular housing preferences. He became convinced that 'most of what passed in the mid sixties for "good housing design" at high densities was in fact a fundamental violation of the lives of those families who had to live in it' and that 'the no-man's-land of communal lift halls and open landscaping was no substitute for the individual backyard in a diverse neighbourhood with pubs and shops.'[21] In the 1940s the political issues in town planning were concerned with housing and environmental principles and national strategy; today these are in the hands of local authorities.

The national focus in fact soon disappeared. In the 1950s the urban authorities and the counties were constantly at loggerheads, particularly over the location of overspill population. This was exemplified by the disputes between Manchester and Cheshire, and Birmingham and Worcestershire. Moreover, local councils, almost irrespective of political composition, could not be relied upon to follow national policy directions; what might seem proper and appropriate from a national perspective did not necessarily appear so to local bodies. Thus strategies for population dispersal were very imperfectly executed at local level, where resistance to loss of rateable value resulted in the failure to disperse industry and employment on a scale to keep pace with the relocation of people. Moreover, only a small proportion of dispersed population found its way to the New Towns or benefited from town development schemes; peripheral growth as far as their boundaries permitted still seemed to suit many local authorities. Higher residential densities also resulted, as with London's high rise estate at Roehampton (1948), which in fact was contrary to policy. Party political machines at local level were strong, and when Silkin in 1947 sharply reduced the number of local planning authorities (the county boroughs and counties only) the effect of this was to increase the political focus of local town planning still further.

Given the power, it was inevitable that local councils chose to exercise it. Some came to engage in town planning in a rather insensitive way, depending on how the council was run. The bureaucratic machine politics of Morrison's London Labour Party was an example of this. The dominance of the inner cabinet was strengthened; indeed, Attlee described the rule of the caucus as 'the nearest approach to a totalitarian state in western Europe'.[22] The Labour Party saw its role as one of management, discipline and coordination, with specific planning priorities inherited and maintained. All this made for some continuity over time but soon led to an unwelcome rigidity and a routinisation of the planning process.

Local authority performances varied greatly. Coventry was notably imaginative; London's work in the 1940s and 1950s was excellent but the impetus was soon lost; many counties maintained good research units, and in the 1960s, such cities as Newcastle, Leicester, Manchester and Liverpool and Cardiff developed constructive new programmes. By the 1970s, however, they were all involved in local community problems, and political scientists have described the nature of the conflict between the local bureaucratic machine and the interests of local people in Newcastle[23] and Sunderland.[24]

The structure of British local government makes no provision for a single identifiable head (in contrast to, for example, the French *Maire*, the American Mayor or the German *Burgomeister*). Political conflict in town planning is thus not personal. Nonetheless, local leaders can be identified who have exercised great influence over the development of their communities: T. Dan Smith promoted the resurgence of Newcastle;[25] Sir Michael Higgs in Worcestershire resisted Birmingham's expansion in North Worcestershire (though accepting and indeed overcoming opposition to the expansion of Droitwich); Harry Watton was a strong leader in Birmingham from 1959–66, and pioneered a number of innovations.[26]

Throughout the 1960s and 1970s, town planning developed pragmatically following new fashions (for example, conservation and improvement rather than clearance and rebuilding) and responding to new problems (transportation planning, for example, where Colin Buchanan had a great influence on ideas for environmental traffic management). Indeed, in the early 1970s a sharp concern for the environment and 'quality of life' introduced a new dimension to post-war town planning. Town planning was now located in the Department of the Environment, and the new questions of pollution and natural resources attracted political comment. From the middle-left, Anthony Crosland observed that 'Environmental goals should be particularly apt for the Labour movement, for they require policies and attitudes which come most easily to a left wing Party – high public expenditure, social control, strict land-use planning, the elevation of community interests over developers' profits, a bias in favour of public transport and a concern for industrial democracy.'[27] Certainly, environmental questions gave rise to political conflicts of some magnitude, as in the case of the siting of the third London airport, which exposed to the full the vested interests and relative political power of those affected.

The urban programme and its aftermath exhibited the most obvious political switch of emphasis. By the mid 1960s the problems of urban deprivation came to the fore in national politics.[28] Poverty was once again rediscovered: Abel-Smith and Townsend in *The Poor and The Poorest* (1965) found that the number of people living below national assistance rates, whether or not they were in employment, had increased from 600,000 in 1953/54 to 2 million in 1960. The new challenge seemed to lie in positively discriminating on a territorial, group or 'rights' basis in favour of the disadvantaged of society (the poor, the handicapped, the deprived, the homeless, ethnic minorities and others). A move towards area-based, positive discrimination programmes had already begun in the United States during the 1960s, when the Headstart, Model Cities and Community Action Programmes and the Ford Foundation Projects were launched. In 1968, the British Urban Aid Programme was announced and over the next few years a number of area-specific developments took place: Community Development Projects, General Improvement Areas, Housing Action Areas, Comprehensive Community Programmes, Six Cities Studies. The various initiatives were bound up with the recognition of local problems in specific parts of our cities, particularly the older inner areas, and those connected with problems of race relations.

Neither the Urban Programme itself nor the other ventures associated with it were built up from any clearly stated set of aims, but the interrelationships became clearer when the problems of the inner cities came into prominence. By the mid 1970s there was mounting evidence that the dispersal of population and economic activity to the post–war dispersed city was posing problems for the inner areas of the old city. Collapses in the base of local employment highlighted other problems of poor housing and disadvantaged groups. Peter Shore's Inner Urban Areas Act (1978), provided for a switch of resources from New Town and suburban growth back to the inner city through partnership arrangements between central and local government. For the first time for many years – indeed perhaps since the late 1940s – a new town planning strategy had been formulated, and its political implications were acute. A national policy was concerned with geographical allocation of resources in a long-term programme; it was regressive by comparison with the strategy of 1946, but then conditions, both social and political, were very different.

Chapter four
POLITICAL APPROACHES TOWARDS TOWN PLANNING

Although town planning has been a major concern of modern British politics, no distinctive political ideologies have emerged in respect of urban or rural society, or the nature of cities and the environment. Distinctive ideologies about these matters have emerged elsewhere to shape town planning aims and methods, but British political life has been and remains much more pragmatic towards the social and environmental possibilities of town planning. The nearest approach to a political ideology of town planning in Britain is in the long espousal of the twin aims of reduced densities and the decentralisation of cities, but this has been as much a pragmatic readjustment towards overcrowding and overconcentration as any distinctive political philosophy about the nature of cities and their social and economic order.

This British pragmatism is in sharp contrast (for example) to the Nazi ideology of the 1930s which was distinctly anti-urban, at least in the beginning of the period, although later the place of the city and its function to help the German war machine was recognised.

Rather more importantly, there is the much longer history of planning in the Soviet Union. Paul White,[1] suggests that the goal towards which Soviet urban planners have been striving for the past sixty years is 'to plan and build cities which, in their form and physical lay out, reflect and mould new social relationships between people in a classless, communist society.' They are pledged to create cities which avoid the ills of inherited capitalism, which instead foster collectivism and cater for equal opportunity in society. Therefore the town planning objective is a city of distinctive form, with a spatial organisation which is quite different from that of the western capitalist city; this is possible because the city develops according to welfare criteria and in the absence of class distinction and, above all, a land market. White goes on to argue that for various reasons Soviet planners have failed to create cities which are distinctively communist in their form and lay out, but this is not to deny that for half a century or more, a well identified political ideology has shaped Soviet town planning.

A different kind of political attitude stems from the anti-urban philosophy to which (reputedly) the American intellectual has been prone, but this has not led to coherent planning policies in the capitalist world. In the social democracies of Western Europe, political determinants of town planning are just as hard to detect, and in Britain the twentieth–century experience reveals no unified set of doctrines. The evidence is that many strands of thought, from opinion to conviction, have threaded their way haphazardly through the political spectrum. Many of the common attitudes towards the city and its problems have surfaced from time to time in different circumstances, appealing to particular individuals and groups for quite different reasons. The political attitudes so demonstrated may therefore be opportunist; and they may also be contradictory.

All the three main British political parties can justifiably claim to have made important contributions to town planning this century. From the Liberals there has been commitment to housing and land reform and an interest in the regional basis of town planning. From Labour there has been an overriding concern for housing conditions and land planning through centralist strategies. The Conservatives have proved a brake on the Left with their commitment to the sanctity of property and deep suspicion of the State encroachment on community affairs. In addition to this, the Conservatives have a refreshing pragmatism, and an ability to work other people's policies if the opportunity arises.

There are perhaps five clear attitudes which have been supported by various shades of political opinion. These may be defined as follows: (1) a determination to reject past conditions and to put things right in the future; (2) a belief that the local and central State should play an enhanced role in community and environmental affairs; (3) an apolitical pragmatism of community and environmental management; (4) a belief that the enlarged role of the State should be reversed; (5) the recognition of the importance of individual leadership in certain circumstances. These different attitudes should not be regarded as in any way exclusive, but their identification helps to build an overall picture of the politics of town planning.

REJECTION OF THE PAST; DETERMINATION TO REBUILD

The Victorians had a love-hate relationship with their cities. They were proud of growth, power and achievement, but horrified by seemingly intractable social problems. The protest literature of the late nineteenth century did much to precipitate political response to the various reform movements, and the Liberal Government from 1905 provided the early basis of the twentieth century welfare state in which town planning found a place. It is interesting to see how the political mind of those years reacted to urban conditions. Winston Churchill, for instance, was greatly influenced by Rowntree's *Poverty: a study in town life* (1901). At the end of that year he wrote to a leading Conservative politician in Birmingham:

I have lately been reading a book by Mr Rowntree called *Poverty*, which has impressed me very much, and which I strongly recommend you to read. It is quite evident from the figures which he adduces that the American labourer is a stronger, larger, healthier, better fed, and consequently more efficient animal than a large proportion of our population, and this is surely a fact which our unbridled Imperialists, who have no thought but to pile up armaments, taxation and territory, should not lose sight of. For my part, I see little glory in an Empire which can rule the waves, and is unable to flush its sewers.[2]

In similar vein were the views expressed by the Prime Minister, Sir Henry Campbell-Bannerman when he received the freedom of the City of Glasgow in 1907. In his speech of thanks he observed:

the concentration of human beings in towns . . . is contrary to nature, and . . . this abnormal existence is bound to issue in suffering, deterioration, and gradual destruction to the mass of the population . . . countless thousands of our fellow-men, and a still larger number of children . . . are starved of air and space and sunshine . . . This view of city life, which is gradually coming home to the heart and understanding and the conscience of our people, is so terrible that it cannot be put away. What is all our wealth and learning and the fine flower of civilisation and our Constitution and our political theories – what are all these but dust and ashes, if the men and women, on whose labour the whole social fabric is maintained, are doomed to live and die in darkness and misery of the recesses of our great cities? We may undertake expeditions on behalf of oppressed tribes and races, we may conduct foreign missions, we may sympathise with the cause of unfortunate nationalities; but it is our own people, surely, who have the first claim upon us . . . the air must be purified . . . the sunshine must be allowed to stream in, the water and the food must be kept pure and unadulterated, the streets light and clean . . . the measure of your success in bringing these things to pass will be the measure of the arresting of the terrible powers of race degeneration which is going on in the countless sunless streets . . .[3]

There was no doubt that the urban condition was a common enemy of the day, and the force with which this view was held, clearly contributed much to a climate of opinion in which town planning could develop.

The same sense of rejection of unacceptable urban conditions, particularly with regard to housing and poverty, has continued to fuel political protest and give strength to those who seek reform. It proved to be within town planning that the machinery for some of these reforms was to be found. Aneurin Bevan, for instance, on being elected a Councillor to Tredegar UDC in 1922, applied himself to such matters as housing, water, health and the beauty of the town. Tredegar's housing conditions were particularly bad; Bevan is quoted as saying 'People were living in conditions not fit for criminals. No doubt horses, especially race horses, were housed much better than some of our citizens are being reared.'[4] He proceeded to fight for the establishment of a proper housing committee and for the maximum use of Government subsidies; as Minister of Health, he initiated a programme of Council building backed by the largest subsidies in British history.

Protest over housing was for a long time the most potent force in reform circles. Sir Ernest Simon was one politician who saw the clear relationship between the provision of better housing conditions and the wider strategic framework of town planning. As early as 1929 he reaffirmed the policy framework suggested earlier by Chamberlain's Unhealthy Areas Committee:

It is impossible to exaggerate the importance of town planning . . . for the proper development of our cities and of the country as a whole . . . The problems of town planning are: where the houses should be built, how amenities should be protected, how transport should be provided . . . How to prevent a continued increase of population in cities like London and Manchester, and to transfer the increase to garden cities, is one of the great problems of the next generation.[5]

The target was still housing reform, and the belief one of 'physical determinism', that an impoverished environment was associated with (or led directly to) an impoverished life. The rejection of the past was fiercest when there was a moral fervour for improvement. In the 1930s this was apparent in the popular mood for slum clearance. Simon (arguing against clearance) advocated instead a policy of building more dwellings at low rent, maintaining that:

it is only in accordance with the general trend of public opinion during the last two generations. We have insisted that every child shall be given decent education; we have insisted on a great extension of public health measures, hospitals, sanatoria, health visitors; and yet the child who grows up in overcrowded conditions in the slums has no real chance. The child is the test. It is the future generation that matters.[6]

Rejection of the unacceptable was intimately related to the concept of an ideal future. Idealism and utopianism fed powerfully into the late nineteenth century stream of ideas from which town planning itself emerged. Dennis Hardy has described the various 'alternative' communities which sprang up in nineteenth–century England – communities of utopian socialism, of agrarian socialism, of sectarianism and of anarchy, and it is clear that they were important expressions of common ideals and aspirations.[7] Howard's Garden City was in the same mould of thinking. A better future was envisaged, in which the evils and philistinism of the machine age were eradicated. This sort of utopianism was also preached by William Morris in *News From Nowhere* (1890). Scientific futurism was reflected in the works of H. G. Wells, but the abrasive violence (which had political overtones) associated with the Futurism movement established by the Italian F. T. Marinetti in 1910 fortunately did not take root in Britain.[8] Instead, dreams about the future of urban Britain remained parodoxically, both pragmatic and romantic. In the inter-war years it was perhaps George Lansbury who best captured the dream of a future Britain in town planning terms. MP for Bow and Bromley and First Commissioner of Works, 1929–31, he was Leader of the Labour Party, during the period 1931–35. *My England* (1934) is a moving book, impractical yet inspired by a love of England (and particularly the east end of London) and by the belief that the way forward was charted by Christianity and Socialism. In a chapter devoted to planning he wrote:

I want to see the electors give a mandate to a Socialist Government which will enable all Britain to be replanned, and replanned so as to give a fuller life for the common people. . . . I do not want Dowlais or Merthyr, Poplar or Canning Town, the Black Country or the coalfields of Lanarkshire, or anywhere else like that replanned. My object would be to sweep away these and similar places. They cannot be improved: any attempt to do that would be a waste of time. The factories with their smoke and muck, the ever increasing slag heaps around every mining and iron and steel area must go.[9]

He hoped for the obliteration of class distinction in housing, ('I would have no West Ends and East Ends') and for the abolition of slums. A National Housing Commission 'would survey Britain, and as labour and materials are available, would get on with the gigantic task of rehousing the nation.'

The rejection of inherited conditions and the striving for an ideal future both owed much to the experiences of individuals. In 1922 the ILP captured almost the whole of Glasgow and the experiences of the urban and economic conditions of that time considerably moulded the political attitudes of the leaders, notably Wheatley, Shinwell and Johnston.[10] John Wheatley left his mark on housing legislation (the Housing Act, 1924 is associated with his name). Thomas Johnston became Secretary of State for Scotland. In his book *Memories* (1952) his attitude towards Scottish unemployment between the wars was unequivocal:

... we were always from 5 per cent to 7 per cent worse. In the period 1932 – 1937 there were 3,217 new factories started in Great Britain, but Scotland got only 127 of them, or one in every twenty five; and during the same period we closed 133 factories, so we actually lost on balance. We had serious emigrations of our healthiest stocks of citizency; we had 300,000 houses without water closet; our maternal mortality was 50 per cent higher than in England and Wales; our infant mortality was 25 per cent worse; our army rejects were 6 per cent higher; control of some of our banks was moving south to Lombard Street.[11]

Not all Secretaries of State for Scotland were particularly energetic.[12] Sir John Gilmour (appointed in 1926) for instance, combined his Cabinet post with the captaincy of the Royal and Ancient Golf Club of St Andrews. The Sixth Earl of Roseberry commented when he left office, '.... didn't make a bad job of that. Didn't have time.' Johnston, by contrast, did much to change a passive stance in Scottish administration to an active one. He tackled the problems of industrial decline by attracting industry north and sought the redevelopment of the Highlands with such measures as the creation of the North of Scotland Hydro Board.

By the end of the 1930s, many of the ideas concerned with the rejection of the past and building anew had assumed some continuity and coherence. For a period of thirty years a certain structure unfolded, which was broadly attributable to the Labour Party. The Party Manifesto of 1918, *Labour and the New Social Order*, presented a programme more or less replicated in the Manifesto of 1945, *Let us Face the Future*, and subsequently carried out by the Labour Government of 1945–51. Lewis Silkin, LCC Housing Chairman, summarised the machinery needed for national planning, in a Fabian pamphlet of 1943:

Immediately after the war there will be a general urge to plan and redevelop our cities and towns, and especially to take advantage of the destruction that has taken place in order to replan those which have been damaged. It will naturally not be possible to rebuild the whole of Great Britain immediately after the war. Preference will have to be given to those areas which have been most sorely stricken and which are more urgently in need of reconstruction, but all such reconstruction must be made to fit into a plan which a Central Planning Authority, under a Minister of National Development, will prepare, and to which all future building and rebuilding will be made to conform. Such a plan must naturally not be static. It must be easy to amend in the light of changed circumstances, and it will be the duty of the Minister of National Development, possibly advised by a National Development Committee, to make necessary changes from time to time. The plan will in many cases not be capable of complete fruition for periods up to as long as half a century, but during that time the Minister of National Development, through Regional or Local Planning Authorities responsible for the detailed planning in their area, must have complete and adequate control of all building which takes place. He must be in a position to prevent the erection of buildings which conflict with the plan. Moreover, the Regional or Local Planning Authorities must be large enough to be able to carry out a comprehensive piece of planning of their area. Unless there is a National Plan and the Regional or Local Planning Authorities are very much larger than the existing ones, post-war planning will be as local and chaotic as it was before the war.[13]

Silkin's prescription was built on the successive pressures to do away with the conditions of the past and to recreate the future. Within two years he was Minister of Town and Country Planning, and for a brief period the idea of national, comprehensive land planning held sway. For the Left, the enemy was class interest:

In the past, planning has consisted merely of telling people what they must not do. It has not been possible to ensure that the things you wanted done should be done, because we have relied entirely on private enterprise, and private enterprise was only prepared, naturally, to provide the development that was needed to make a profit. If planning is to serve the public interest in the future and put all the agreed principles into effect, it has to be free of this sectional interest . . .[14]

The way forward to a new future was confidently prescribed – good homes, good conditions of work, good opportunities for recreation and a good community life. National land planning was one of the keys to such a future.

CHANGING ATTITUDES TOWARDS THE STATE

The twentieth century has seen important changes of emphasis in public attitudes both towards local government and the central State. These changes have had important consequences for town planning, sometimes encouraging its growth, and sometimes, as in recent years, severely damaging its prospects. In Britain, town planning is very much a public service, an activity of the State, and its development has been dependent on broad assumptions relating to the place of Government in social, economic and environmental affairs.

At the beginning of the century, local government had a tolerably good image in urban affairs. Apart from the big exception of housing, it had proved competent and welcome in many areas of city management. Public service on local councils was held in high regard and local government seemed capable of taking on a range of social services in addition to its nineteenth century duties. Neville Chamberlain painted this picture during his speech at the Second Reading of his Local Government Bill in 1929:

Local government comes so much nearer to the homes, and therefore to the hearts of the people, than any national Government can. To them it is something friendly, something familiar, something accessible. It is all that to them, and yet it is above them. They regard it as standing as a guardian angel between them and ill-health or injustice, and they look upon it, too, as something in the nature of a benefactor and a teacher in want. They come to it for advice. They feel confidence in its integrity. They look to it because it has ideals which they understand, and they approve, and because it is always helping and teaching them to rise to higher things.[15]

This expression of confidence helped town planning when the post war planning system was being devised. The essential relationship between central and local government could be retained and indeed strengthened precisely because of the confidence which rested in local authorities. Had local government been weaker, and had not the spirit of local democracy been built into effective machineries of government at this level, British town planning would have followed a different course. The benevolent guiding hand of a local Council was a sure rock on which town planning could rest. With the experience of Manchester and Wythenshawe behind him, Simon could argue that since the nineteenth century:

the City Council has been steadily grappling with one evil after another. Now, after the efforts and experience of over a century, we have learnt how to design, build, and equip a really good working class house at a relatively low cost, how to plan an estate in detail so as to preserve its natural beauties, how to plan a city as a whole so as to provide cheap and quick transport from home to place of work, to separate factory areas from dwelling places, to provide good schools, healthy open spaces and playing fields. We know now what a town ought to be like, and we have a good deal of experience as to the right methods of guiding and controlling its development.[16]

This was a powerful statement of a local authority's obligation and capacity to control, to steer and to plan. At national level, however, there was not this confidence. The concept of planning was virtually unknown, even to the socialist vocabulary, until the first Soviet Five–Year Plan was inaugurated in 1928.[17] Even then in non-socialist circles, the idea of further public sector extension in such areas as land planning, economic affairs, and transport was regarded with hostility. It took a financial crisis, the collapse of the second Labour Government, a whole decade of cautiously shifting attitudes and finally a World War, for political sympathies to change and swing to the Left.

We should of course recognise that the first approaches to economic planning came quite early. The political diary of Thomas Jones,[18] a Deputy Secretary to the Cabinet, shows that as early as 1924 there were attempts to set up machinery specifically designed to initiate economic planning. A Committee of Civil Research emerged in 1925 and in 1929 the Labour Government set up an Economic Advisory Council.

The failure was one of institutions rather than ideas, and institutional reform was necessary in the 1940s. In the meantime, political ideas changed, particularly on the right. During the 1930s the problem was widely identified as that of 'economic and social progress in a free and democratic society', which was the subtitle of Harold Macmillan's very influential book, *The Middle Way* (1938). Macmillan recognised the merits of capitalism and socialism; he also recognised the need for a combination of the public sector with private enterprise. He envisaged an economic structure in which provision was made for different forms of ownership, management and control of industries and services at different stages of development. The safeguard against totalitarianism was in a new approach to planning: 'the secure bulwark against reaction or revolution is an economic system that can satisfy the moderate needs of men for material welfare and security, while preserving at the same time the intellectual, social, and political liberty essential to human progress in a wider field.'[19]

By this time, informed opinion found scarcely credible the idea that economic systems could be self regulating in such a way as to be ultimately beneficial to the community. Intellectually, the case for planning in the sense of State direction of community affairs had already been won, and over the next few years town planning itself was to benefit. In political terms it became acceptable, as it was realised that a strong centralised State would work in conjunction with democratic local government. Simon made the telling assertion: 'if British democracy makes up its mind, it can within the next two generations make the cities of England once more places of beauty in which it is good to be alive.'[20]

By the early 1940s, determination to reject the unacceptable conditions of the past, went hand-in-hand with the recognition that the State had an important role in environmental affairs. Both these views were increasingly articulated by the Labour Party, and the promises for post-war recovery (such as those we have quoted from Silkin) were fed from this source. By itself, this group would not have been sufficiently powerful, and it was necessary for the arguments for an enhanced State role to come from other directions. As has been shown very important political shifts became possible in war-time Britain because of the erosion of entrenched attitudes. The British political centre moved markedly left and a wider State role was less and less questioned, and more and more urged. Land planning and the planned creation of beautiful cities became a general expectation.

POST-WAR POLITICS

A broad consensus of opinion existed in relation to town planning, from the war-time years until roughly the beginning of the 1970s, notwithstanding political conflicts over betterment. Town planning became almost a-political, and was broadly supported by the three main political parties. There were different emphases, but essentially the same pack of cards was being shuffled.

For the Conservatives, Peter Walker, a former Secretary of State for the Environment, has written in support of state powers to control land use: 'We have made many mistakes in the pursuance of such a policy, but nothing like the mistakes that would have been made had free market forces been allowed to operate.'[21] Keen to pursue policies of social reform that would eventually eradicate poverty and squalor, he was much influenced by Jack and Robert Kennedy's attempts to awaken America to their inner–city problem in the 1960s. Walker himself set up studies of certain towns to formulate guidelines in order to help local authorities develop a total approach to environmental management.

For the Liberals, Grimond confirmed in the 1960s a commitment to macro planning and regional resurgence, particularly with a view to restoring a national balance, by taking growth away from London and the South East.[22] His passionate belief in a democratic society made him hostile to large corporations and bureaucracies, and more sympathetic to small-scale community structures: 'The Bureaucrats at their worst have replaced the landlords and tyranical employers as the incubus people feel upon their backs. The new Kremlins, those vast office blocks frowning down on the serfs, who support them, are indeed the successors to the medieval castles and what goes on in them is equally unknown to those outside.'[23]

For a long time there was broad agreement on political matters regarding the role of the State in matters of town planning. Labour's objectives in the 1930s (abolition of poverty and the creation of a social service state; a greater equalisation of wealth; and economic planning for full employment and stability) had been powerfully underwritten during the war years. Planning became a central feature of post-war recovery and there was a good deal of consensus over the nature and extent of State intervention. However, there was a gradual fading of the post-war hopes of public planning. Town planning was one of the areas where impetus was lost and consequently, disillusionment set in. Anthony Crosland was one who read the early signs.[24] He acknowledged the post-war promise: 'Brilliant, imaginative town-plans were to re-create our major cities. . . . Above all the Town and Country Planning Act was to be a sure defence against the vulgarities and atrocities of the past.' But progress had been slow and now there was indifference, selfishness and philistinism. The Labour Party could still take a lead in this clash of values:

It would, in the judgement of history, do more for Britain by planning the City of London than by planning the chemical industry, and infinitely more by abolishing hanging than by abolishing the tied cottage. It has a favourable background and tradition for assuming this role – the influence of William Morris, its long-standing belief in social as opposed to private values, and the tender, respectful feeling for culture that characterises the educated working class.

So town planning was part of the struggle for cultural values. But Labour thinking remained very traditional, wedded to eradicating the evils of the 1930s. Gerald Fowler (a Labour commentator, then at the Ministry of Technology) more or less repeated what Lansbury had said, thirty years earlier:

Few Socialists will wish to bequeath their heirs a country in which towns and cities sprawl and haphazardly coalesce; where more time each day is spent in commuting to work; where the Englishman's home is his castle because he must turn away from and shut out urban ugliness; where there are neither the facilities nor the time for him and his neighbour to lead a vigorous social life; and all this while the remoter regions continue to stagnate. Yet this could be the future which faces us, unless we take action now.'[25]

Nonetheless British politics were changing, as Crosland had observed. Peter Shore was also aware of change.[26] In November 1956, he was chosen by the Halifax Labour Party as their prospective candidate, and this led to regular journeys from his home in Harlow to the West Riding of Yorkshire. He was struck at the differences, 'between two industrial revolutions, between two centuries'. He thought that mid-century politics were now 'about human relationships more than social amenities, about power rather than poverty'. He argued that new problems for socialism were now bound up with the growth of corporate power. Twenty years later, as Secretary of State for the Environment, he was responsible for making a major switch in resource allocation, in order to tackle the problem of the inner cities. During the mid 1960s, manufacturing employment in the major conurbations began a rapid decline, accompanied by a remarkable net outward migration of population from the inner districts. As MP for an inner London constituency he was well placed to launch a new policy. He has since argued:

No one should claim that our large inner cities were ever places of obvious visual attraction, but much post war development has been ugly, brutal and insensitive. Today the inner city policy proceeds in a very different intellectual, professional and social climate than existed 20 or even 10 years ago. The tide now flows strongly in favour of conservation: there is a greater respect for the past, a greater humility about constructing a Brave New Social World in which everything is vast and everything is new.[27]

Thus the Left (but not exclusively the Left) have maintained important attitudes, concerning town planning and public policy, resting on old approaches perhaps, but pragmatically grappling with new problems. The deep rooted vision of Blake's 'Jerusalem in England's green and pleasant land' is still there, and the phrase was repeated by Roy Hattersley as he reviewed the achievements of his Sheffield City Council in matters of housing, smoke control and social facilities.[28]

STATE WITHDRAWAL

During the late 1970s the apolitical consensus was broken. Arguments gained ground against the ultimate beneficence of the State and in favour of the removal of the fetters on private enterprise. Town planning was inevitably involved. The imperfections of local government in dealing with community issues, particularly in housing matters had long been a source of criticism and this fostered a general belief that local authorities were failing to direct aid to those in greatest need and that they were multiplying the difficulties of those they were intending to serve. In economic and other affairs it was abundantly clear that the State held no monopoly of wisdom, and centrally directed State programmes of economic, social, fiscal or land planning were disquietingly imperfect. It was argued that planning, with all the bureaucracy that was needed to underpin it, was costly, inefficient and wasteful.

The limitations of town planning, long concealed, now came into the open and could not be protected by the soft-centred idealism of earlier years. Town planning was good at little things, often perhaps inconsequential; it could regulate environmental detail very well, but could do relatively little to achieve the grand futures long promised. Above all, it was better at stopping things happening, than creating things new. Town planning, long held to be benevolent, now had critics which saw it as positively malevolent.

The issues surrounding this new sharp twist in political affairs will be considered in more detail in chapter 6. I am concerned here with the changed town planning climate under the Conservative Government of 1979 and the new Secretary of State, Michael Heseltine. Outlining his philosophy to the Summer School of the Royal Town Planning Institute in 1979, he made it clear that he had no intention of wrecking the planning system developed over the last forty years; nonetheless he believed 'we have ended up with a system which tries to do too much. We have ended up with a hierarchy of planning, planners and plans in which the simple objectives have become obscured and for which the actual and imposed costs have soared.'[29]

He wanted a streamlined process, and argued that structure plans should not be 'a vehicle for displaying every conceivable matter of interest to a county council'. New plans should not require 'another round of vast surveys, or expensively collected extra statistics'. Unnecessary public sector controls were being scrapped: 'the apparatus of planning control seems to have grown bigger and more complicated. It seems to have become ponderous and detailed.' Delays in decisions about development control must be reduced; he wanted to see 'a change of attitude towards the purpose of development control – a change of attitude by the planners who administer it and the councillors who are responsible for it. . . . This country, in economic terms, cannot afford the manpower involved in a system which in some parts can be negative and unresponsive. But above all, we cannot afford the economic process of delayed investment, whether commercial, domestic or industrial.'

This link with macro-economic considerations provided the practical point in the philosophical argument for 'rolling back the frontiers of the State'. Heseltine's underlying belief was that Britain was experiencing a steady decline in economic fortunes – 'an inexorable slide down the economic league table'. He did not suggest that town planning or the planning system was the main factor but it was 'one contributory factor among many'. Britain was facing a last opportunity to regain a significant place in the world of economic power. The planning system should play a role in this by being able to produce results quickly and efficiently and not stand in the way of creating the conditions favourable for economic growth. His attitudes towards small businesses and the development of vacant land were already common knowledge; in 1980 proposals for Free Enterprise Zones were announced.

This was a speech from a Town Planning Minister (or Secretary of State) very different in tenor and content from any of his predecessors. It was a break with the past, shaped by a new approach to the role and influence of the State. Local government administration was now on a different course, and the wider remit of town planning could not escape. Regional economic planning, for example, lost the only institutional base it had when the Economic Planning Councils were abolished in 1979.

Sir Keith Joseph, another senior Minister who has poured scorn on our present planning system, also prefers the freedom of individual action to unnecessary control by the State. In a paper to a joint conference of the RIBA and the Civic Trust in 1974 he argued:

Clearly it is right that we should try to protect our environment and we cannot do that without a measure of planning. We do need a system that restricts the sprawl of cities and preserves areas and buildings of historic or aesthetic importance and declares conservation areas and protects trees. We do need a system that broadly allocates land uses and densities, that plans communications, that makes indispensable appraisals when location decisions have to be made. We should recognise that the control of advertisement hoardings has been a success and should be retained. We do need health powers against irredeemably bad housing. We do need a system that subjects some proposals to scrutiny, however difficult the definitions may be at the margins. And should there not be a right of appeal to the councils and the courts on all these points? But do we really need the immense apparatus that we have at the moment – the arbitrariness, the bureaucracy, the delays and the expense?[30]

From a former Minister of Housing and Local Government, Joseph's paper represented a template for the new political philosophy against the established planning orthodoxy. 'We have had no planning for 4,000 years and planning for forty. Are memories so short that we already regard detailed planning as part of the eternal order of the universe? There is indeed a grave danger that we may react to the failures of the past planning by taking an ever larger dose of it in the future.' The crudity of this argument did not prevent some other telling swipes. Land shortage may be 'born of demographic and economic expansion, but it is nurtured by planners' … 'The delays and tergiversations of planners are responsible for waste of good building land'... 'Too much power and responsibility is taken by governments'... 'The results of planning and rent control [are] a monument to the extraordinary combination of ignorance and arrogance which have characterised the collectivist approach since the war.' Sir Keith continued with a swingeing attack on planners:

It is not only that the pursuit of town planning aims intensifies land shortage, prolongs delays, increases devastation, imposes rigid lifeless solutions; it is not only that town planning makes the artificial shortages that lead to the fortunes that feed envy; it is not only that the ambitious system of town planning leads to long administrative delays with heavy concealed costs all round on top of the visible costs of a big bureaucracy; it is not only that any system leading to such wide disparities of land values must offer temptation to corruption; it is that town planners and architects are as fallible as the rest of us and the more power we give to them the greater the errors that will be made when they are wrong.

A political philosophy of this kind promised a very different future for town planning, which, so far shaped by Chamberlain, Macmillan, Silkin, and Crosland, embarked on a significant change of course.

PERSONAL ASSOCIATIONS

Outside these broad currents of political philosophies there have been important examples of personal contributions fed by attitudes of loyalty or commitment to local situations, or personal convictions as to particular courses of action. The post–war planning history of Coventry for example, owes much to the long serving Planning Committee Chairman, George Hodgkinson[31], who in his autobiography claims that he 'saw the challenge of reconstruction in four dimensions [consisting of] the adherence to a master plan comprehensively developed, provision for pedestrian and vehicle separation, a public share in the equity of development and planning for people by participation.'[32] The reign of a leading local politician at Newcastle, T. Dan Smith, although was shorter was more dramatic. In the 1960s his city was in the forefront of planning experiment and determination. Retrospective bombast cannot entirely overshadow his sense of mission:

. . . in Newcastle I wanted to see the creation of a 20th century equivalent of Dobson's masterpiece, and its integration into the historic frame work of the city. If this could be achieved, I felt, then our regional capital would become the outstanding provincial city in the country. The method of development, as I saw it, was to make good existing deficiencies by a new central area redevelopment . . . I was determined that Newcastle would not accept just any architect whom the developer might wish to impose on it. I felt it wrong that when a city was beginning to take care to ensure that its public buildings were of the highest standard and best design, it should show less concern about its central redevelopment. The best of our national and international architects were to be commissioned.[33]

Today, Newcastle has a redesigned central area surrounded by urban motorways; the Eldon Square indoor shopping complex and the Tyneside metro complement the graceful curve of Grey Street and 'Tyneside Classical', the Victorian city centre planned and administered by Clayton the Town Clerk, laid out by Grainger the speculative developer and designed by Dobson the architect.[34]

At national level perhaps only one post-war politician has left an individual stamp on town planning and environmental matters. Duncan Sandys was Minister for Housing and Local Government from 1954 to 1957 when he introduced the famous Green Belt circular of 1955. This was very much a personal initiative, lacking Departmental support, but it met with widespread acceptance. Faced with the impressive evidence of the London Green Belt, provincial local authorities found a ready place for the greenbelt concept in their own strategic plans. For the county authorities in particular, this device of land reservation (which had already received the stamp of approval from the technical expert) was of considerable political significance in their battles with the cities.

In 1957, Duncan Sandys founded the Civic Trust. His civil servants and some Ministerial colleagues advised against this: to set up an independent organisation which would prove to be a pressure group against his own Department seemed the height of folly. But the Prime minister, Sir Anthony Eden, cautiously agreed and Sandys duly became President. Improvement schemes at Norwich, Burslem and Windsor were quickly implemented, and a variety of facelift schemes to protect and enhance the environment soon received popular support. Further campaigns: free planting schemes, the removal of eyesores, the presentation of Civic Trust Awards, extended the work of the Trust. The Lee Valley Regional Park Authority (east London) was established by Act of Parliament following the formulation of a Plan by the Trust. A Private Members Bill (introduced by Sandys) became the Civic Amenities Act (1967), which introduced the concept of the Conservation Area, extending legal protection from individual buildings of quality to whole areas of architectural or historic interest. At the international level the Trust plays a leading part in *Europa Nostra*, a federation of conservation organisations in European countries (founded in 1963) of which Sandys is President. The age of personal political initiative in town planning matters, beyond the framework of the statutory system, is clearly not dead.

Chapter five
PLANNING AND POLITICS IN PRACTICE

Harold Wilson has recounted the story which he heard towards the end of the Second World War, second hand from a minister who had just come from Cabinet:

There were six or seven subjects on the agenda. The earlier ones were on straight war issues, relations with allies and similar topics. At 1.00 p.m. Winston Churchill closed his Cabinet folder and lit another cigar. Sir Edward Bridges drew his attention to the fact that there was still one remaining item.

It was town and country planning. The determination of those days that we should not go back to the 1930s had inspired Beveridge, the Cabinet White Paper on full employment, and also the three basic reports on town and country planning by Uthwatt, Barlow and Scott. Winston had created a minister of town and country planning, Mr W. S. Morrison, (later Lord Dunrossil). Starting the post-war housing programme after six years in which hardly a house had been built depended on decisions about planning, betterment and compensation.

W. S. Morrison had assessed these reports and was presenting his conclusions. Winston was not amused. 'Ah, yes', said he. 'All this stuff about planning and compensation and betterment. Broad vistas and all that. But give to me the eighteenth-century alley, where foot-pads lurk, and the harlot plies her trade, and none of this new fangled planning doctrine.'

If Morrison had been wise he would have said that he fully agreed with the Prime Minister; that he assumed the Prime Minister was approving his paper, that he assumed the Cabinet agreed, and that in all his planning he would take care to make full provision for narrower vistas and alleys for appropriate activities, such as those mentioned. Winston would have said, 'Quite right, my boy, you go ahead.' Instead, Morrison stammered out, 'I take it, then, Prime Minister, you want me to take it back and think again.' Winston replied, 'Quite right, my boy.'

Morrison went back without any guidance about redrafting and did not emerge before Cabinet for some months – a vital loss of time before Britain's post-war housing programme could effectively begin.[1]

This amusing, though perhaps apocryphal, tale illustrates what many people may feel today about planning and politics: that it is all a rather shady area of dubious decision taking and a matter of horse trading between vested interests. On the other hand, we have the contemporary evidence of Andrew Blowers, academic and Chairman of the Environmental Services Committee of Bedfordshire County Council between 1973 and 1977, who has described how planning power and influence is actually exercised.[2] For some politicians, planning appears as 'an esoteric, impenetrable activity. It is often not a matter for party political controversy but a quasi-judicial procedure in which cases are treated on their merits in supposed conformity with certain planning principles.' But Blowers confirms that 'planning, as part of the State's organisation, mediates various interests, seeks to achieve consensus, and attempts to coordinate and guide activities to avoid future conflicts.' Significantly, Blowers' book, which deals with the politics of local planning policy, describing the power possessed by professional planners and politicians and how that power is distributed amongst them, is entitled *The Limits of Power*.

Previous chapters have shown that these characteristics of limitation have indeed been common enough. A major reason for this is the inherent instability of the British planning system, structured as it is with three inter-active elements. In making this point, one observer, Peter Hall, sees at the heart of the system a bureaucracy, 'generally massive and well established', concerned with policy and programme maintenance; it is inherently conservative except when political pressure creates the demand for rapid expansion and new policy initiatives.[3] At its edge are activist pressure groups seeking to exert leverage on professional, political and controversial issues. The third element is composed of politicians who seek to accommodate the demands of these groups. It is in this context that the planner actually operates. The dilemma is that if a professional ignores political behaviour, his decisions will be unrealistic and incapable of implementation. On the other hand, if he is always compromising in face of political pressure, he ceases to be a decision maker, and his planning role is thereby atrophied.

The inter-action of these three-fold elements, the political, the professional and the community, provides the context within which British planning actually operates. The planning system in practice is the result of tensions within and between the three parts, and at any time the policies or strategies followed, and decisions taken, will be determined by the supremacy of one element over the others. Sides taken may vary: the professional bureaucracy may be supported by pressure groups in the community (as with National Parks or preservation of old buildings for example) or fiercely attacked by them (motorways or forms of public housing). It all helps to explain the flux and uncertainty which we have noted earlier; and it is therefore instructive to look more closely at the operation of the planning system from this point of view.

THE INTERACTIVE SYSTEM

Political values

British political traditions with regard to planning have been schizophrenic: we have come to like the idea of planning, but we also have a liking for pluriformity. Attempts to combine the two attractions have created difficulties. There have been times when a control philosophy has been uppermost, while at other times (more frequently) a permissive, evolutionary view of change has been favoured. The distinction between planning control and pluriformity is sharp (and can be seen in the different forms of planning which can be recognised at different periods) – broadly speaking one is planning to change the system, whilst the other is planning to maintain the *status quo* through affirmation or gentle correction. These fundamental differences, observable within the political values of Britain and the West, provide the context for some strange vacillations over time in approaches to problems.

It was in the context of this tension, between planning control and pluriformity, that the British New Town scheme was executed. The New Towns programme of the later 1940s was underpinned by a set of ideas and attitudes which were politically explicit so far as they concerned community life. The New Towns Committee, chaired by Lord Reith, enthusiastically endorsed the concept of a 'balanced community', balanced not only in terms of work and services to overcome the unwholesome evil of the day, commuting, but also in social terms. The point was 'one of class distinction . . . if the community is to be truly balanced, so long as social classes exist, all must be represented in it. A contribution is needed from every type and class of person; the community will be poorer, if all are not there, able and willing to make it.'[4] Reith went on to show that a social mixture would only be attained through careful attention to the design of the built environment: the skilful location of sites for houses of all classes and the early provision of buildings for various amenities were to be the physical tools for the creation of a socially homogeneous community. The intention, favoured politically and supported professionally, was a social experiment, a joint programme of social and physical engineering. 'Members One of Another' is the significant inscription on the Coat of Arms of Harlow Corporation, reflecting the aspirations of a consensus community. The sociological and other assumptions underpinning the approach did not go unchallenged for long, but the British New Towns programme continued to harness political and professional support for a range of idealistic design elements, long after the first flush of enthusiasm articulated by Reith. Today we look at Cumbernauld, for example, perched high on its hill top between Glasgow and Stirling and marvel at the set of ideas, relating both to its high density residential environment and multi-storey central shopping complex, which gave it its birth. In the 1980s we find it very difficult to put much faith in such dramatic ideas of design or forms of social engineering. Social scientists today point to the constraints which have operated both on the structure and management of New Towns. In respect of Stevenage, Mullan claims to identify three sets of actors (politicians, industrialists and pressure groups associated with protest movements) who have served to confuse the New Town ideal.[5]

But New Towns can be built with other reasons in mind; other political objectives may be followed. The New Towns of Paris in the 1960s are a case in point, as examined by Goursolas.[6] General de Gaulle's ministers drew up a development blueprint in 1964 for constructing new urban centres of two kinds: restructured centres in the already urbanised but under-equipped inner suburbs and New Towns in the outer suburbs. Two axes of development were identified, one on the north and one on the south of the Seine, both designed to have the effect of breaking up the monocentrism of the Paris urban area. Eight New Towns followed (two in the northern suburbs, three in the west, two in the south and one in the east), but a revision in 1969 reduced the total to five; and since then there has been sharp criticism of their failure in terms of job creation, house construction and transport links. But it is the political interpretation which is interesting. Goursolas asserts that the state apparatus rebuilt by de Gaulle in 1958 was pervaded by a ruling class which consisted of the Gaullist State and the technocrats, who came from the 'grandes écoles'. Together they tried to reform the country and break with the past, as embodied in the power structure of the Fourth Republic. In this context the objective of Gaullism was to re-establish the State's presence and break the strength of the 'red belt' in Paris. The New Towns policy 'could not be otherwise than a function of the changing relations of class'.

By comparison, British planning programmes are rarely so political (if Goursolas is correct), and in any case political influence changes over time. Housing policy is a typical example. Niner and Watson observe that the chosen role of central government is to act not directly, but indirectly.[7] In Britain, government has not taken control of the housing system, preferring to see others responsible for implementation (local authorities, the private sector, building societies and private landlords). Government has on occasions created special agencies to implement its policies, as with the Housing Corporation, but such an initiative has been rare. There is, therefore, a multiplicity of objectives in housing policy, and different political motives are apparent at different times and at different levels of housing policy. In 1919, the introduction of council housing was at least in part due to fears of working-class action against housing shortages, just as the introduction of rent control in 1915 was the result of a rent strike in Glasgow. In the years after 1945, political intervention in housing policy has operated through the use of the construction industry as an economic regulator – both to boost and to cut house building. Housing is of course a political issue: the number of houses to be built and the selling or not of council houses, are both examples of housing policy which have gyrated according to the priorities of particular parties in office. The low salience given to housing as an issue of the day in the general election of 1979 was very unusual in recent British politics.

There is one issue, above all perhaps, where a political viewpoint has had a very strong effect on planning policy, namely interference in the land market. The questions of compensation and betterment, development value, land tax, land nationalisation and compulsory purchase have produced expected battle lines between the political parties, as we have seen in 1909, 1944, 1947, 1966 and 1975. We are particularly fortunate to have the Peacetime Histories on Environmental Planning which reveal the detail of political debate on these matters. Cullingworth has described the twists and turns whereby systems were devised both by Conservative and Labour Administrations to provide a solution to the problem of compensation and betterment which was practicable in a society wedded to the principle of private ownership.[8] In retrospect, Cullingworth is struck by 'the extraordinary amount of heat engendered by arguments over a relatively narrow field of disagreement'. Highly technical issues gave rise to political difficulties, and political objectives led to technical problems. Furthermore, political decisions taken at a particular time became constraints on subsequent change. Hence politicians found themselves defending policies about which they privately expressed unease; their established positions were difficult to abandon; differences were exaggerated, and viewpoints became entrenched.

Neither does the issue promise to lie dormant in any way if the recent writing of a land economist, Donald Denman, is to be followed.[9] In a vigorous defence of the protection of private property rights and a denunciation of the State's performance in post-war land planning, he asserts that the general aim of a land policy in this country should be to ensure the unfettered working of a free land market. In his view, there is no case for special land taxation, and taxation of development value in land is bad taxation. There should be strict limits to public acquisition of land because 'a society is free in the measure in which its land is free and privately owned'. The extent to which these views are politically adopted or rejected will determine important planning policies, so far as land is concerned, in the 1980s and beyond.

On the other hand there have been and still are certain planning areas where political consensus obtains. Public concern for the environment is one example. Sandbach reminds us that there was overwhelming support from all the major British political parties in creating comprehensive environmental legislation during 1973 and 1974 when Control of Pollution Bills were introduced by both Conservative and Labour parties.[10]

The profession

It would be misleading to regard professions as a homogeneous occupational group, sharing a unique character and destiny. Indeed, to the social scientist they present very different profiles. T. J. Johnson, in his study of professions, thought they were 'Janus–headed': 'they provide both a structural basis for a free and independent citizenry in a world threatened by bureaucratic tyranny and at the same time themselves harbour a threat to freedom.'[11] An imputed altruistic motivation on the one hand may be contrasted with a seeming inability to exercise social responsibility on the other.

The planning profession in this country, represented by the Royal Town Planning Institute is no exception, amply demonstrating its set of shared beliefs throughout the century. Broadly speaking they have related to qualitative improvements in the physical environment, attainable in part through the wise control of, or direction over, private acts of development. But the profession is not homogeneous, and in any case such an abstracted view is interpreted in decision taking at many levels and at various intervals in time. Professional planners have many backgrounds and experiences and are exposed to different influences: the planner trained first as an architect in the 1940s will tend to act and think differently from the planner trained first as a geographer or sociologist in the 1960s.

Even within one specialist area of planning there will be different ideas and approaches. An academic lawyer, Patrick McAuslan, has made this clear with regard to planning law, where he sees three competing ideologies: the traditional common law approach, that the law exists and should be used to protect private property and institutions; the orthodox public administration and planning approach to the rule of law, namely that the law exists and should be used to advance the public interest – against the interest of private property, if necessary; and the radical or populist approach, whereby the law should be used to advance the cause of public participation.[12] The ideology of public participation is becoming the ideology of opposition to the *status quo*, whereas the ideologies of public interest and private property are the ideologies of the *status quo*. The planning system in practice has so far largely reflected the ideologies of a governing elite, for the most part bound to existing structures of government, society and institutions; the alternative ideology is in opposition to this and aims at a more open and participative form of planning.

Professional pluralism is also reflected in the threefold mix of professional, judicial and political traditions – 'a troika of irreconcilables' according to another academic, Regan, which because of its diverse and mutually contradictory elements has stretched the British land use planning system to the utmost.[13] A system which relies on professional, judicial and political processes all at the same time, can sometimes produce the same answer, but it is more likely that it will not. The three processes have an inbuilt tendency to produce differing results over time. Until the Second World War, the planning system was basically judicial; planning schemes were mainly bundles of rules governing the use of pieces of land. After 1945, the system shifted in emphasis from judicial to professional, and planning experts became dominant. The current planning system has become political in that the community is more able to express opinions and even directly influence policies, while judicial insistence on the protection of individual interests or guidance of technical expertise has become less powerful. Nevertheless, all three traditions continue to make up the internal struggles in British planning: the extent to which it is, or should be legally, professionally or politically-centred.

In recent years the planning profession has taken a number of stances which are avowedly political, departing strongly from a professed apolitical line earlier in its history. One of these is its commitment to planning aid from 1972 onwards by both the RTPI and the non-professional, but propagandist body, the Town and Country Planning Association (TCPA) which has a Planning Aid Officer. The idea of planning aid has taken root from the various attempts to bridge the gap between planners and the public, particularly in the recognition that not all persons are equally able to defend themselves. A service was envisaged whereby, independent of any central or local government body, attempts would be made to give free advice, information and assistance on planning issues to individuals, community groups and voluntary organisations. Over the years, a need for planning aid has been established and the feasibility of a service, staffed voluntarily, has been proven through a number of local experiments.

The community

A significant feature of the last two decades is the growth of environmental societies, and the rise in their membership, which has taken place during the 1960s and early 1970s. Sandbach reports that of 605 local amenity societies in existence in 1974, only 15 per cent had been founded before 1958.[14] Such bodies are now firmly part of the planning system; key influences shaping attitudes and exerting political pressure. Their origins and methods of working are rarely unravelled, but they are in fact of some importance for the planning process itself. One useful study we have is that of the early campaign for a National Park in the Lake District, by Sandbach, who emphasises the role played by the Friends of the Lake District.[15] In fact the formative years of the early 1930s were shaped by a complex interplay of personalities, organisations and events, and the secretaries of the Friends and the Council for the Preservation of Rural England were crucially placed to influence events through the timing, structuring and control of meetings.

Each operated closely with certain key figures, while professionals like Abercrombie mediated in the middle. The activities of the two bodies contrasted strikingly. CPRE operated closely with the Department of Health and other government bodies; it did not so much campaign, but rather mediated, between groups with conflicting interests. It was the Friends who adopted increasingly aggressive tactics, and succeeded in achieving most of their objectives.

In more recent years there has been the action group approach from Marion Shoard, a vigorous protester against the destruction of the English countryside by new farm technology.[16] She advocates organised public pressure at grass-roots level through Countryside Action Groups. She maintains that, having formed the group, organised speakers and discussions, and tackled the media: '... nothing will impress ... more than a little action at the battle–front. Impose your Countryside Action Group's presence on a stretch of the countryside ... Get to know the local authorities, water authorities, landowners. Pester all of them. Hold meetings, demonstrations, marches and bring-and-buy sales to acquaint local people with your thinking.' The advice flows thick and fast. Take on the National Farmers' Union (NFU) on their own terms. Study the farmers' methods. Bombard political parties and trades unions with the group's findings. 'Think and act. The activities of organised enthusiasm are constrained only by the limits of the imagination of the enthusiasts.' It so happens that the sympathies of many planning professionals are with this landscape protest. National politicians however, are allegedly indifferent, and in any case they are subject to strong appeals from other lobbies, notably those of farming, motoring, military and occasionally industrial pressure groups. New land-use planning directions are possible in this climate of considerable agitation, as suggested by the introduction of the Government's Wildlife and Countryside Bill (late 1980), and the subsequent controversy surrounding it.

Pressure Groups are thus part of the mechanism whereby popular attitudes are mobilised over time, political decisions are reached, and directions of planning forged. But planning policies can later come under fire when popular attitudes fail to be maintained and turn course. These changes in values help to explain the 'great planning disasters' of our time, as Peter Hall describes them.[17] With regard to London motorway proposals, for example, he believes the main reason for failure was 'without doubt, a massive shift in values and the expansion of these changed values into the political arena . . . When the motorway plans were unveiled in 1965–7, both political parties, together with the media and a wide spectrum of public opinion, were publicly and enthusiastically in favour. By the time they were abandoned, in 1973, there was hardly a voice left in support.' The same about-face can be seen in respect of Concorde and airport location: 'it is now condemned because of a massive shift of values against this kind of technologically speculative measure and in favour of resource conservation and environmental protection. But when the critical Concorde decision was made in 1962, very few people publicly cared either about noise around airports or about fuel conservation.'

There is abundant evidence that the history of British planning in recent years has been profoundly influenced by the mobilisation and articulation of attitudes by public pressure groups. The majority of these groups have fallen into two types: those which broadly relate to environmental issues and those which are connected more to the politics of community action in respect of unwelcome forms of urban redevelopment.

Gregory has recounted in detail five studies of pressure group battles in conservation and government: Oxfordshire ironstone, Holme Pierrepoint and the power station, the Cow Green Reservoir, Bacton and North Sea gas, and the Abingdon gas holder.[18] In 1971, he observed that 'in the last twenty years or so "amenity" has regularly and conspicuously come to be part of the stuff of conflict between developers and their opponents.' Ten years later the situation shows few signs of resolution, and there are some classic *impasses* where the processes of government have simply failed through prevarication and indecision. The image of effective British local and central government is somewhat tarnished for example in respect of the Oxford Inner Relief Road/Christchurch Meadow controversy, which goes back to 1923.[19]

Another instance of vacillation, by central government at least, is the question of the Third London Airport, which brought to a head the issue of amenity considerations versus 'rational' planning based on other criteria. The Roskill Commission of Inquiry, reporting in 1971, recommended that the airport should be located at Cublington, Buckinghamshire. This was after an extensive review and cost benefit analysis of alternative locations, but Colin Buchanan in a Note of Dissent objected to all three inland sites that had been considered, and recommended that the airport be located at Foulness on Thames-side in South Essex. He emphasised the following: the importance of a comprehensive approach to planning; the need for environmental protection; the significance of major locational decisions as instruments of social policy; and the need for careful judgement in handling sophisticated methods of analysis. Foulness was renamed Maplin and for a period was favoured by Government. But the debate continues over strategic locations and their environmental significance, and now the controversy centres on the expansion of Stansted for the third airport.

The capacity of environmental questions to attract popular lobbies is obviously very great. Kimber and Richardson have brought together a number of examples from their research.[20] Many of them reflect the common characteristic that the environmental lobby tends to be middle class, but there are instances of activity in working class areas, such as the Swansea housewives' blockade of the United Carbon Black Factory in February 1971, and the union pressure leading to the closure of the Avonmouth lead and zinc smelter in January 1972. Elsewhere, and at different times during the last quarter of a century, with varied class and interest support, other pressure groups have been active. The conservation of historic environments assumed significance in the 1960s when cities such as York, Chester, Chichester and Lincoln were threatened by the ravages of the motorcar. Architectural Heritage Year (1975) and more recently the European Campaign for Urban Renaissance (1981) have both maintained conservation of the built environment at an elitist, professional and technical level, with rather vague political support.

Other issues have been more specific, as for example, the power lines across the South Downs, which concerned the County Councils and the Central Electricity Generating Board, secured the involvement of the Sussex Downsmen and led to the formation of Action Committees. Problems over the lines of motorways have led to sharp disputes. A good example is the M4 in Berkshire, which led to clashes between a host of action committees, the Kennett Valley Preservation Society, the CPRE, independent experts and the Ministry of Transport. Another all-embracing amenity issue was Manchester's water supply in the 1960s. In 1961, the City decided to promote a Private Bill to abstract water from Ullswater and to create a reservoir elsewhere. The Bill was debated in the Lords and defeated on Second Reading, opposition being composed of national and local amenity organisations, local landowners and private individuals.

In other cases, environmental objection has been to forms of pollution. The National Smoke Abatement Society, an active propagandist for clean air, had its efforts rewarded in the 1950s. The great London fog of December 1952 led to the setting up of the Beaver Committee on Air Pollution the next year. A Private Member's Bill sponsored by Gerald Nabarro fell with the General Election of 1955, but the Clean Air Act (1956) soon followed – a remarkably successful measure which has largely abolished industrial fogs, led to enthusiasm for cleaning of buildings, and has given higher winter sunshine figures in urban areas for a century or more. A combination of pollutions, air, noise, and visual, is threatened by juggernauts. Public opposition to heavy lorries has been orchestrated by leading conservationist organisations and voluntary associations concerned with road safety, who have also pointed out the increased social costs incurred by heavy vehicles.

The environmental lobby continues to be a vigorous one. Graham Moss writing on 'Britain's Wasting Acres' will not be the last in a long line of those who call for understanding and care for the environment, with greater public responsibility towards land, knowledge about land, and education in the care of land.[21] There is no lack of evidence to show that environmental issues arouse fierce passions. Public opinion has been particularly sharp against the motorcar and its capacity to destroy homes: over 250 for York's inner ring road, over 1500 for Cardiff's Centre plan and 15,000 for London's projected motorway box. Nationally, there have been famous protests against new airports and airport extensions, motorways, oil rig construction sites, power stations, nuclear waste disposal, coal mining, and other threats to the environment.

Pressure groups may often enter directly into local politics on a town planning matter.[22] In 1970, in the Greater London Council elections, 85 candidates from the Homes Before Roads group contested seats in 27 boroughs on a platform of opposition to the Council's motorway plans. In 1974, in the London Borough elections, representatives from the environmentalist Save London Action Group appeared on the ballot in a number of places. In the Essex County elections of 1973, the leader of the Anti-Maplin Defenders of Essex was elected on a platform of opposition to the proposed Third London Airport. European Green Parties have perhaps a more permanent record. In Britain the formation of the Green Alliance in 1978, which aims at the reshaping of British political thought within an ecological perspective, suggests possible new developments.

Local pressure groups may be even more vigorously mobilised on local issues of urban renewal. In the early 1970s, Davies[23] in respect of housing renewal in Newcastle, and Dennis[24] in Sunderland both described an all-too-common feature of the planning machine, an unholy conspiracy between professional and political insensitivies riding roughshod over local housing interests. But the classic ingredients are seen in those grand plans for urban redevelopment which fail to take account of the complexity of local feelings. Ravetz, for example, recounts the case of Chesterfield market, where local opposition was mounted against the local authority's scheme to demolish listed buildings and an open-air market in favour of a developer's five-acre shopping complex.[25] Between 1956 and 1973 the proposal progressed remorselessly through the statutory stages, but it was finally shelved in 1974 after a protest march of several thousand citizens and a petition signed by over 30,000 persons.

An even better example is that of the redevelopment of Covent Garden. The decision to relocate the produce market plunged the area into a decade of intense planning and political controversy. The move, which occurred in 1974, gave rise to problems not only in terms of land use, but also employment, and community life. The first GLC plan which was the subject of a Public Inquiry in 1971, though it included some conservation work, proposed to redevelop much of the area for the purposes of hotels, a conference centre and offices together with housing and open space. In view of the fact that Covent Garden was an area of great diversity and mixed uses, this Scheme was far–reaching in its proposed changes. Pressure soon mounted against the Plan and in July, 1972, Lady Dartmouth resigned her chairmanship of the GLC Covent Garden Committee, unable to work for a project in which she no longer believed. In 1973 the decision of the Secretary of State (Geoffrey Rippon) in respect of the Public Inquiry was to endorse the general objectives but to recommend substantial modifications to be made with full public participation. In fact, the effect was to damage fatally the Plan's intentions. The Labour Party victory that year in the GLC elections led to a very different plan being prepared, with housing, shops and light industry changing the balance of proposed land uses.

The case of Covent Garden is highly significant. It is evident that in the interplay of actors and interests, the local community became assertive, the press showed an interest, there was political reaction, and the planners found themselves regarded as public enemies. A bizarre coalition of conservationist pressure groups emerged, with radical activists allied to conservative, aristocratic, elitist preservationist groups. Terry Christensen has told the story from the point of view of the Covent Garden Community Association, which he believes was 'the cutting edge of the sword that slashed the 1968/71 plans to shreds'. Certainly, it was highly skilled in street by street organisation, using the media, and adopting the public inquiry as a forum.[26] The press caught on to the story, which it presented complete with stereotypes: the nasty developer, the haughty architect, the sleazy politician, the insensitive bureaucrats and planners.

Christensen makes some general points, about the planners' role as technical experts, which are generally applicable to redevelopment schemes of the 1970s. He believes that as professionals, the planners were largely concerned with the built environment, thinking and planning in terms of the city as a whole, rather than in terms of its parts; in other words they began with a grand strategic view and worked downwards, rather than adopting the reverse approach. With bureaucratic inertia they were resistant to change, and a different plan had to be forced upon them.

The strong political bias of the Covent Garden Community Association was soon apparent. They had to learn to deal with decision makers by developing skills in technical language, communication and organisation. There is no clearer example of the ideological perspective of a community organisation influencing the course of a particular planning scheme. Christensen recounts that the GCA's

predominant bias is in favour of the working class and elderly residents of Covent Garden and the protection of their community. They are unwilling to compromise with the planners, the developers, the property owners or the middle class residents of Covent Garden, unless the compromise is distinctly to their advantage. They are disdainful of the chic restaurants and trendy shops that seem to be taking over Covent Garden. But they are not entirely anti-business, for they are enthusiastic about shops that serve residents, such as butchers and ironmongers, and about light industry that provides residents with jobs.

The GCA's left-wing politics inclined them to ideas of community self-help and neighbourhood self-determination, leading inevitably to a clash with the planning system which accepted the capitalist use of land and the rights of private property and made a commitment to the maximum economic potential of land use, rather than the development of working class housing and its related service sector.

Covent Garden may be a special example, but today's planning news is composed of myriad such action protests against (in the eyes of some) unwanted development. Reliance on representative democracy in the local council, or on planning experts whose professionalism once (but not necessarily any longer) made them above politics, has broken down. The question now is: whose values are being protected, and by whom?

THE PLANNING SYSTEM AT WORK

Any planning system operates within the available political processes. These will be determined by differing political cultures and ideologies, the institutional frameworks of government (national, regional and local) and the arrangements for decision making, both public and private, that affect the various policies which are followed.

To explain the political processes Goldsmith has summarised the five models which illuminate the different approaches.[27] First, the institutional model sees political processes as largely subservient to the institutional, constitutional and legal framework of the country concerned; in Britain, the local authority is largely dependent on central government, and the pattern of interactions between these two levels of government, and between governments of the same level strongly determine what actually happens, particularly in services and functions. Second, there is the community power model; this focuses attention on the decision-maker and the extent to which decisions are controlled by the few, or influenced by the many. Attention therefore is drawn to the processes of local decision making, and its dominance by different actors; we can distinguish between those who hold formal positions of political power, as elected representatives, and those who may exercise power by virtue of social or economic influence. Third, there is the model which might be described as a political response to environmental change, an approach stimulated in the 1970s by a recognition of 'systems', whereby the political system responds in a self–correcting or adaptive fashion to changes outside it. A fourth model emphasises the role of individuals and their values; this has been strongly influenced by developments in urban sociology. A recent variation was the 'urban management' thesis which saw the various managers of the urban system (councillors, officials, and all those controlling resource distribution and access to facilities) as being the real determinants of policies and their outcome. Finally, there are the Marxist models, again emanating from urban sociology; these maintain that the differences in service provision, life chances and access to resources stem from the process of class exploitation which continues in the consumption process outside work just as much as it occurs in the production process.

Each of these models has its attractions, but each by itself is incapable of offering complete explanations. All, however, say something about power, institutional arrangements and interaction and they provide important perspectives for understanding the operation of the planning system. It has become increasingly fashionable to see the process of policy making as a relatively closed one, with power concentrated in the hands of an elite, with the consequence that planners with responsibility for land management, housing and various aspects of welfare, have come under sharp attack. But it is more perceptive to explain the planning system at work as the result of the interplay of three value systems representing politics, professions and bureaucracy, and the community. All are heterogeneous, all may change direction over time and none has primacy over the others for very long. The public sector especially is diverse within itself, and the history of many planning episodes has been determined by the internal disputes of sectional interests.

The Official History on National Parks reveals the differing view points held by Ministers and Departments, after the Hobhouse Committee Report (Cmd 7121) was submitted in 1947, and both before and during the passage of the National Parks Bill through the Commons.[28] There were particular difficulties between the Treasury and the Ministry of Town and Country Planning; on more than one occasion the Chancellor, Sir Stafford Cripps, was brought in to enforce the trimming of expensive sails. The Minister found his own Department of Town and Country Planning very apprehensive about the proposed National Parks Commission: how far would its powers and functions downgrade the importance of a new Ministry? The Minister, Silkin, had to tread a wary path through the biases of political colleagues: some wanted him to go further on the question of compulsory acquisition of land. Hugh Dalton was one of these; he argued: 'we shall have no peace around the Peak until we have paid off the Dukes.'

The public sector is enormously varied within its institutional structures, and this is the cause of many planning weaknesses. I have written elsewhere about such imperfections of regional planning in Britain, regarding the situation in the West Midlands since the war.[29] The present state of central/local relations works against any coherent regional policy, except in the short term. There are antagonisms both within the Department of the Environment and between Whitehall and the Regional Offices. There are misunderstandings between Government Departments and their varied fields of activity such as economic affairs, transport and environment, all exacerbated by quirks of personality, policy and ambition. There are jealousies within and between the local authorities, as they jockey for positions out of self-interest: Shire Counties versus Districts, Metropolitan County versus Metropolitan Districts, and Birmingham versus anyone else. The coordination of physical and economic planning at regional scale has proved especially difficult: it could not be otherwise, bearing in mind that it has rarely been possible to achieve consensus over objectives except at the most general level – and even then in periods of economic growth, and not retrenchment, as now.

The planning system at work is therefore complex. The elements are internally heterogeneous rather than homogeneous, and the interaction between the elements will often depend on the strength and tactics of key actors, rather than the logic or rightness of any particular cause. This is true of any period of planning history this century.

Sheail, for example, has given three illustrations from inter-war Britain when political, professional and electoral factors produced certain planning initiatives.[30] The first was at Eastbourne where downland protection became a major issue. A newly elected councillor advocated local authority purchase of the crest of the Downs above 270 feet, to protect it from housing development. A local Bill was promoted and 4000 acres were eventually secured, but at a somewhat higher cost than was originally envisaged. The Council was later attacked for extravagance. The second example was at Woodbridge in Suffolk where the issue was a by-pass. The initiator was the East Suffolk County Council, who, aided and abetted by technical professional support, encouraged the setting up of an advisory joint planning committee and the preparation of plans by which the countryside could be protected against undesirable housing encroachment. The third example was a local authority response, first by local plan and then by planning scheme, to the public nuisance of shacks and caravans on the Lincolnshire coast around Mablethorpe and Skegness.

Most information on the roles of the various actors in the planning process comes from the post-war period, because in our contemporary years urban social and environmental policy has become so extensive. This has enabled recent commentators on urban change, McKay and Cox, to identify five major sets of political actors: parties in central government, organised professional and economic interests, protest movements, central government bureaucracies and local government bureaucracies.[31] The importance of each has varied according to particular policy areas. Parties in central government, for example, have had strong influence in housing and land values, but little or no influence in matters relating to urban transport or inner cities. Organised professional and economic interests have been active across the board, although most of all in housing, where expert opinion has been widely influential. Protest movements have had their strongest effect on urban transport, with little direct impact on policy elsewhere. Central government bureaucracies have had widespread influence, although much of it has been deadening and constraining. Local government bureaucracies have played an important bargaining role *vis à vis* central government. It is therefore a complex scene in which the transmission of ideas from one set of actors to another assumes great importance – not only between the political parties and the vested interests of organised groups, but also from external services such as academic or other expert opinion.

In the context of this framework there are many hundreds of case studies available to illustrate a typically thorny planning question, from the perception of a problem to the mobilisation of resources to tackle it. Housing is the longest standing field of controversy. One example, researched by Crosby, is the renewal of the Jericho district of Oxford.[32]

Jericho is largely a nineteenth century working class housing area. Deterioration of the older housing set in before even the First World War, and a long period of neglect came to a head in the late 1950s. Another part of Oxford, St Ebbe's, was largely demolished between 1953 and 1963, an experience which was the cause of much local bitterness; and one which politicians did not wish to repeat. An alternative policy, gradual renewal, was consequently preferable to politicians and their officers. Some redevelopment of the most obsolete of dwellings was necessary and this led to hostility of the local residents, particularly when, following detailed surveys, the proportion earmarked for demolition rose to an unexpectedly high level. A familiar story then unfolded, with public anxiety and allegations that the Council was attempting to conceal information. Gradual renewal was found to be more problematic than it appeared, as the absence of a fixed, agreed plan inevitably led to community uncertainty and suspicions. The use of compulsory purchase orders was resented; prices paid for property varied widely and the reasons for the discrepancies were not fully appreciated. The Residents' Association found itself locked in combat with the Council. Environmental improvement schemes such as street closures and paving, which would have been applauded by professional peer groups, were denounced by local residents as inappropriate. Meanwhile, the community itself changed and Jericho underwent some degree of gentrification as higher income groups moved in.

All these aspects of British planning reveal the inevitability of compromise. There is no better example of this than rural planning, where the interests of access, amenity, preservation and agriculture all have to be accommodated. The British countryside has at least three different roles: it is an area productive in food supply, timber, minerals and natural resources; an area to be lived in; and an area for recreation. The points of planning dispute are the results of conflict within and between these roles: the drowning of farmland in the form of a reservoir for urban water; the taking of Grade I agricultural land for gravel extraction; new farm buildings, destructive of scenic value; the preservation of moorland or wetlands to preserve established ecology systems; veto on building development in the interests of scenic beauty, and so on. All these issues produce sharp antagonism between vested interests, and no one more jealously safeguards the countryside than the preservation lobby, as witnessed in the perpetual struggle in National Parks between what is seen to be of local or national importance.

The CPRE has been a vigorous defender of its interests – too much so for it to be warmly welcomed by those who find its objectives single minded. A former Chief Planner at the Ministry of Housing and Local Government, J. R. James, is said to have composed a mock Grace for a CPRE dinner:

> Lord, we thank thee in thy Grace
> For bringing us to this beauteous place;
> But one more thing, dear Lord, we pray,
> To keep all other folk away.

The ardent fervour of the access propagandists has made them uncomfortable bedfellows in the rural scene, clashing sharply with those who advocate conciliatory or contrary policies. This struggle has gone on for the last half century and more, as witnessed by the political clashes over the Access to Mountains Act (1939), and the various National Park issues since the war. In the early 1930s, the access issue came to focus on one area, Kinder Scout in Derbyshire. Much of the land on the Kinder Plateau belonged to the Duke of Devonshire and was jealously guarded for grouse rearing. Land around neighbouring Bleaklow was owned by Sheffield Corporation, which again restricted access for similar reasons. There had been a long history of individual trespass on the shooting preserves, but the question assumed a new significance with the advent of mass hiking and the emergence of radical ramblers' organisations, of which the Communist-inspired British Workers' Sports Federation, with fifteen branches in Lancashire and two in Sheffield, was to play a prominent part in 1932. The historian, Lowerson, has recently recounted how on an April Sunday that year the Secretary of the Lancashire BWSF led a group of between 150 and 600 ramblers up to Kinder Scout from the village of Hayfield.[33] A mass rally demanded open access, low fares, non-militarism in rambling groups, cheap catering, and the removal of restrictions on open air singing. They were repulsed at the top by a group of eight keepers, reinforced by temporary wardens; they returned, singing revolutionary songs and the ringleaders were arrested. All five were subsequently imprisoned at Derby Assizes for periods of between two and six months. The issue of access was brought into the arena of public debate, thus providing the background of the various Access to Mountains Bills in the 1930s, and ultimately the pressure for National Parks in the 1940s.

Another struggle of the present day, is that to preserve England's celebrated landscape – its 'patchwork quilt of fields, downs and woods, separated by thick hedgerows, mossy banks, sunken lanes and sparkling streams.' As described by Shoard, this landscape is under sentence of death, and the executioner is not the industrialist or property speculator but the farmer, traditionally viewed as the rural custodian.[34] The allegation is that hedgerows and hedgerow trees, downs and heaths, woods, ponds, streams, marshes and flower-rich meadows are being systematically eliminated by new agricultural methods. In this case the fight is not so much against a planning system and its destructiveness, but rather seeks to impose one, in order to employ a measure of control against the forces of unwanted change.

RECENT PLANNING ISSUES

The internal working of town planning can be further illustrated by reference to issues which have attained public prominence over the last fifteen or so years. The political, institutional, professional and pressure group influences on planning and planning-related policy are many. The more complex and historically rooted the problem, the greater the interplay between the forces.

Housing

Housing matters have had the closest association with town planning since the beginning of the century and the links between the two functions of local government remain strong. Housing policy has often implied planning policy; housing improvement and the means to attain it has often been at the heart of planning objectives.

Housing is one of the most important community resources and so it is not surprising that political, professional, and community feelings run high. The difficulty, as Alan Murie and others have observed, is that housing is a vital element in social policy, yet social policy objectives are often remarkably vague (improving the quality of life, or the provision of decent homes, or help for people in need, for example).[35] Another difficulty is that problems change over time, and because of the time lag in political appreciation of changing circumstances, some rather foolish statements have been made. For example, in 1953 Harold Macmillan, then Minister of Housing, claimed that 'many local authorities should be able to solve their housing problems in five years or so'. In 1972, Julian Amery, Minister of Housing and Construction, was convinced that 'if we really set our hands to it, we can beat the problem of the slums and unsatisfactory housing within a measurable time'. Earlier, in 1969, Kenneth Robinson, Minister of Planning and Land, forecast that by 1973 there would be a margin of one million more houses than households in the country, a surplus which promised the end of the national housing shortage and spiralling house prices.

What in fact has been happening? The record of the last thirty years or so, is one of undoubted improvement. For England and Wales, the total housing stock increased by 5½ million dwellings in the quarter century 1951–76. In the same period the number of households increased by 4.3 million, and a crude deficit of about 800,000 dwellings in 1951 was turned into a surplus of half a million. The impressive rates of new housing construction, the demolition of old houses, and the improvement of the ageing stock, has led to a steady decline in the number of households living in unfit or substandard dwellings. There is also less over-crowding and sharing of dwellings; the number of overcrowded households fell from 664,000 in 1951 to 150,000 in 1971, and sharing households declined from 2.8 million to one million.

To achieve these results, housing policies have followed a number of different paths. There has been encouragement of owner occupation; subsidised public sector housing, with rent rebates and allowances; rent control in the private sector; and improvement grants for the upgrading of dwelling stock. Various measures of State intervention have been developed in response to the conviction that market forces alone can provide neither an adequate stock, nor its fair distribution. Intervention has been necessary especially to ensure decent housing for low income households. The welfare objectives of housing policies, namely a minimum level of housing provision for all, in order to obviate high rent and housing costs falling on the poor, have found general favour.

Obviously there have been political twists and turns in all this, as Lansley's recent review of housing and public policy has shown.[36] These have been well demonstrated in attitudes to rent control. With the Rent Act of 1957, the Conservatives introduced widespread decontrol measures to revive the private rented sector. In 1965, Labour reintroduced rent control in the form of rent regulation, instituting the concept of 'fair' rent designed to give landlords a reasonable rate of return from letting. Another example is the question of public spending: the attitude of the Conservative Government 1970–4 was different to that of the Labour Government 1974–9, and sharply different again to the Thatcher Administration of 1979 onwards. In all these periods, public investment in housing followed disparate patterns.

Housing problems remain, and indeed will always be with us while housing resources are imperfectly allocated. The problems will be both rural and urban. Rural questions, typically those of holiday homes, tied cottages and various problems related to shortages and high cost of accommodation in up-market commuter villages, have recently been the subject of investigation by Dunn and others.[37] But notwithstanding the clear evidence of rural housing deprivation, the biggest problems are concentrated in the urban areas. It is too easy to be complacent about our qualitative improvements over recent years. Reductions in public expenditure on housing have shown how fragile is the balance within our system. By 1990 one third of the dwelling stock of this country will be at least 100 years old; this poses a great necessity for investment in improvement, maintenance and modernisation, but this measure of investment is simply not forthcoming. Households are still in need;

there is a housing shortage; overcrowding still exists; substandard conditions prevail – all to an excessive extent.

Often the problem bursts into prominence with a particular issue. Homelessness is an example. In 1966, the television play *Cathy Come Home* portrayed the descent into helplessness created by lack of access to housing. Degradation of this kind attracted widespread publicity. Squatting is an explosive political question and it is likely that this and other housing problems will be exacerbated over the next decade. Britain's performance compared with other European countries already looks disappointing. Shelter, the organisation which campaigns on behalf of the homeless and the badly-housed, asks 'what kind of nation do we want to be? Basically the question is as simple as that. We are in imminent danger of so neglecting our housing stock that wholesale bulldozing of communities will again become inevitable. We are already imposing intolerable pressures on a minority of our people by denying them decent homes. We are at risk of becoming the slum of Europe.'[38] Certainly, for the town planner, the country's housing problems must be high on his agenda: impoverished neighbourhoods and environmental squalor; the bleak design of many local authority estates; the unlettable housing stock and the associated urban decay; the difficulties associated with tower block living; the limited housing tenure choice and the difficulty of moving from one tenure group to another; and the number of people with special housing needs – all these problems are priorities.

Housing problems are both national and local, and an area-based approach to housing is as important as a set of country-wide objectives. There is clear evidence that housing stress is spatially concentrated. Holtermann's study of urban deprivation, using data from the 1971 Census, revealed the problems at conurbation level.[39] Using six indicators of housing stress, she identified Enumeration Districts in which there was a concentration of housing problems. Among the conurbations, Clydeside consistently came out the worst – except from the point of view of shared dwellings, which remains largely a London phenomenon.

The housing field therefore contains some classic ingredients both in the formulation and execution of public policy, and in the reaction of community pressure groups. In Britain, a substantial role has developed this century for both public intervention and the private market. Government has set standards, provided subsidies, exercised control over housing agencies (for example, the building societies) and made direct provision of housing. These measures have resulted in the strong link between town planning and the twentienth century concern for welfare.

Metropolitan strategies

Up to the early 1970s, British town planning policy followed a broadly decentralist model of population dispersal from the big cities. Although publicly sponsored, New Towns and Town Expansion Schemes provided a relatively modest contribution to the migration of the total population, a strongly running tide of both suburban development and the expansion of country towns has ensured a very different population distribution map from that of earlier years. Congested, over-compressed cities have finally given way to loosely–structured, amorphous, metropolitan cities of truly regional scale. The first reports of the 1981 Census have revealed the considerable extent of the changes which have taken place even in the last ten years. In England and Wales, the metropolitan counties and Greater London all lost population between 1971 and 1981. The decrease for inner London amounted to 18 per cent; exceptionally, Kensington and Chelsea recorded a 26 per cent decrease, but Hammersmith and Fulham, Islington, Westminster, Lambeth and Southwark all had above-average figures. The metropolitan cities, Manchester, Liverpool and Birmingham recorded losses of 17, 16 and 8 per cent respectively. The loss for Newcastle upon Tyne was 10 per cent. In all cases the beneficiaries have been the urban fringes and certain rural areas.

But this scale of suburban and peripheral development has now reached a point which suggests that lasting impoverishment in the inner, older areas of cities might ensue, unless policies of positive discrimination in their favour are urgently and consistently applied. The extent of population exodus (highly selective in its socioeconomic and demographic composition); economic collapse in the city cores resulting from a combination of economic recession and technological change; the incidence of widespread deprivation; and the heightening of racial tensions – all these problems have come together at one point in time, and while it would be quite wrong to focus unduly on one geographical area, nonetheless it is the inner city which captures the attention.

The emergence of the inner-city problem in the 1970s illustrates particularly well how the State comes to intervene in complex environmental, social and economic affairs, in response to an absence of initiatives elsewhere, and pressure from various sources. It also demonstrates that once a particular set of policies have been adopted, the State can do very little about strategic metropolitan problems which are both complex and large-scale.

The introduction of urban aid in 1968 marked the beginning of Government response when the Home Secretary, James Callaghan, noted that despite general affluence 'there remain areas of severe social deprivation in a number of our cities and towns – often scattered in relatively small pockets. They require special help to meet their social needs and to bring their physical services to an adequate level.'[40] This observation came at a time when problems in the inner, older areas of cities were being tackled from other directions, particularly with area-based, positive discrimination measures. These were directed especially towards education (of Commonwealth immigrants), and housing, where rehabilitation policies were favoured instead of demolition. Commentators today believe that Enoch Powell's 'river of blood' speech of April 1968, which warned against continuing immigration, provoked a political response. The Prime Minister, Harold Wilson, announced in May of that year a decision to embark on a new and expanded Urban Programme. The announcement was followed by the setting up of an inter-departmental working party to consider what form the programme might take. Eventually the Urban Programme, run by the Home Office (rather than the Ministry of Housing and Local Government, and its successor the Department of the Environment) took shape, dispensing aid to areas which showed high incidences of overcrowding, large families, immigrant concentration, children in need of care, and other aspects of need. The remarkable feature was the broad political consensus: the Conservative Home Secretary, Robert Carr, was an equally enthusiastic advocate of this form of selective aid, and he set up the Urban Deprivation Unit in the Home Office.

A number of initiatives were crowded into the first half of the 1970s. The Community Development Project (CDP) was set up by Callaghan in 1969. The first four areas selected were in Coventry, Liverpool, Southwark and Glyncorrwg (West Glamorgan). The remaining eight were at Oldham, Batley, Paisley, Cleator Moor, Newcastle, Tynemouth, Saltley (Birmingham) and Canning Town. The initial thinking behind the CDP was that deprivation was related to, and in part caused by, three things: inefficient local authority service provision, lack of communications between resident and the authority, and the absence of any critical seeding agent which might be capable of generating community self-help projects.

Existing political formulae were increasingly rejected by the CDP teams which favoured methods based on theories of conflict. Explicitly Marxist frameworks of analysis and prescription led to the demise of the CDP. First, the Home Office allowed local authorities to decide their commitment to the future of individual teams, and finally the CDP Information and Intelligence Unit was closed in 1977.

Meanwhile, Peter Walker, Secretary of State for the Environment, launched his Six Towns Studies in 1972. He had been attracted by the Shelter Neighbourhood Action Project (SNAP) in the Granby District of Liverpool, a study which recommended a 'total' approach to the problems of such deprived areas. Through contracts with professional consultants, two types of studies were undertaken. In respect of Oldham, Rotherham and Sunderland, the focus was the management of towns and the decision–making structures which dealt with urban environmental problems. Elsewhere, Liverpool, Birmingham and Lambeth were selected for Inner Area Studies.

By the mid 1970s, inner-city problems had a high political salience. Substantial research findings were now available, and pressure for new policy initiatives came from academic and interest group quarters (Shelter and the Child Poverty Action Group, for example). But inter-party politics had a small role to play, and new lines of direction seem to have been devised within Government, with little reaction to pressure exerted from outside, except perhaps of certain academics. The White Paper *Policy for the Inner Cities* (June 1977) spelled out the Government's recognition of the inner-city problem, and its commitment to arresting the decline by means of a set of unified proposals. The Inner Urban Areas Act (1978) followed, with new funding and provision for partnership arrangements.

There is no doubting the scale of the problem. As Andrew Kirby has pointed out, the inner city contains 7 per cent of the British population (3.8 million), 14 per cent of the unskilled workers, 20 per cent of the households in housing stress, and 33 per cent of the Commonwealth immigrants.[41] Unemployment is running at twice the national average, employment opportunities are contracting at over twice the national average. Up to ten times the national proportion of families live below the Supplementary Benefit poverty line.

Coherent policies to combat these problems have been slow to emerge. One critic, Lawless, describes the government's inner-city policy as 'neither viable nor sensible' and 'a typically British, and almost certainly ineffective, compromise'.[42] Faced with the nature of the problem, the nature of British politics and bureaucracy, and the nature of British planning, this verdict should not surprise us. The problem is immensely complex and the factors responsible for decline lie outside the inner city, being part of the spatial restructuring which is taking place at metropolitan scale. This comprises an economic down-turn at the centre and a selective migration of population from the inner core to elsewhere in the regional city. The acuteness of the problem is relatively recent, and the severity of the collapse in the 1960s and 1970s took many people by surprise. The manifestations of the problem – bad housing, poverty, environmental deprivation for example – have traditionally been tackled independently and therefore the approach has been fragmented, both by pressure groups and professional bodies. (The one professional body capable of offering a coordinating role, the RTPI, was not particularly well placed to do it, because of its uncertainty in dealing with non-spatial phenomena.) So the problem fell to politicians and civil servants, and here perhaps Lawless is a harsh critic. All political initiatives are compromises, within the one party, or between parties, and between national and local interests; thus it may be said that Peter Shore's legislation of 1978 was as big a departure as could have been managed; the switch in financial resources and the new partnership arrangements promised much, and it will be interesting to see whether subsequent Administrations continue the strategy for long.

The inner city provides the context for some recent planning initiatives: for example, Partnership projects funded under the Urban Programme, the setting up of Urban Development Corporations for London's docklands and Merseyside, the Glasgow Eastern Area Renewal (GEAR) Scheme, and the designation of Enterprise Zones in hard-hit areas, designed to take advantage of financial incentives and the simplification or withdrawal of administrative regulations (including planning). But plans to regenerate the inner city have been prejudiced by the deepening economic recession, cuts in public expenditure and the erratic application of local authority rate support grants which have disadvantaged many urban areas. In the meantime the inner-city problem will not go away; indeed it is deepening due to perceived disadvantage over housing, unemployment and environmental decay, with no escape route through education and with the added difficulties caused by racial tension. In this context violence on the streets has erupted in Bristol,

Brixton, Southall, Liverpool Toxteth, Manchester Moss Side and elsewhere. The explosive tensions concerned with the return of mass unemployment are now high on the political agenda, as suggested recently by Friend and Metcalf in a flamboyant, left-wing analysis, *Slump City*: 'the crisis of social and political control generated by concentrations of people existing on the margins of society is set to become both more widespread and intense.'[43]

Regional planning

Since the war there has been a considerable measure of political and professional agreement about regional policy, based on the seemingly unassailable decentralist arguments contained in the Barlow Report of 1940. War-time experience of the planned location of industry, together with a populist determination not to repeat the regional economic problems of the 1920s and 1930s, led to a consensus approach which sought to transfer mobile manufacturing employment from the South East and Midlands to areas of economic disadvantage (and commensurate high unemployment) in North and West England, Scotland and Northern Ireland. In a period of modest but reasonably sustained national economic growth some redistribution of industry could help to cushion the consequences of long-term structural decline in heavy engineering, textiles, shipbuilding and coal. Until the mid 1960s unemployment rates were remarkably low, even in the worst hit regions and for many years the problems which had beset Britain in the inter-war years were defused. Perhaps based on bad economics, in that Britain failed to let its economy expand in those areas which were most suited to it, consensus politics were content to underpin the principles of planned decentralisation in the interests of social justice.

The strength of regional policy varied with the vigour of political will, the circumstances of time (expansion and reflation) and increasing pragmatism which continued to permit industrial expansion in the more favoured regions, contrary to established policy. The method continued the same however: the requirement of an Industrial Development Certificate for building industrial premises above a certain size (in order to control the location of new plant), the designation of Development Areas which were to receive special assistance, and a combination of financial and other inducements to achieve a new pattern of employment distribution. Some spectacular Governmental interventions saw major industrial locations determined in the car industry (Linwood and Halewood, for

99

example) and iron and steel (Ravenscraig) and in other sectors too. During the 1960s a brief attempt to control office development was made, supplementing a longer phase of voluntary encouragement for office dispersal via the Location of Offices Bureau.

Regional policy peaked in the 1970s and a deteriorating national economic situation demanded changes in approach by both Conservative and Labour Governments. John Mawson has suggested that reappraisal stemmed from three factors.[44] First, policy instruments such as financial incentives and floorspace controls are less relevant in a period of minimum or nil economic growth; second, it became more difficult, politically, to justify transferring jobs from one region to another (the West Midlands became particularly vociferous as it went from the category of prosperous to disadvantaged region in the space of a decade); and third, the policy of diverting jobs in a period of high national unemployment, lost validity. The level of assistance to unfavoured regions has been sharply reduced, particularly since 1978; Regional Economic Planning Councils, set up by George Brown, were abolished by Michael Heseltine; and the whole basis of post-war regional planning has been undermined, so much so that at the present time Britain can scarcely be said to have a regional policy.

The full implications of this new situation have yet to be realised. While a significant number of new jobs have been created in the depressed areas (perhaps 325,000–375,000 in the last two decades), these regions failed to build up economies capable of self-sustaining growth. The regional economies are still dominated by declining basic industries, and this suggests that much more will have to be done in order to make local economic environments capable of adapting to local economic circumstances, rather than being dependent on shifts of national policy. All this is of significance for town planning. So far the town planner has been the hand-maiden of the macro-economic strategist, scarcely able to contribute to economic debate but paying lip service to the principles of decentralisation (often against all the evidence). If the focus is now inter-regional rather than intra-regional the town planner may have a more obvious role to play in attending to local government conditions and joining in a multi-professional lobby for economic regeneration. Political and popular support may return to the idea of comprehensive planning within the regions, with objectves of economic regeneration related to social purpose and the physical form and appearance of cities.

Transportation

Town planning has long been associated with the problems of road traffic. London's traffic congestion and the attractions offered by the promise of a circulatory ring road pattern were being discussed by town planners well before the First World War. Although traffic regulation continued to be a matter very much for the police, city building necessitated considerable attention to highway design, and in consequence the reconstruction years of the 1940s and 1950s inevitably brought planning and transport together. This bond was strengthened when research showed that land use and traffic movement, expressed in terms of journey to work, were intimately related.

The continued explosion in car population (the number of vehicles on British roads doubled between 1951 and 1961) brought severe problems to central areas where congestion became acute. But old street patterns were being refashioned at a time of central area renewal, and the circumstances were ripe for a new approach. Vehicle-pedestrian segregation had long been admired in some cities as, for example, in Coventry's central area, and there was a greater appreciation of the need for environmental protection from the dangerous, polluting effects of the car. Colin Buchanan's Report *Traffic in Towns* (1963) put great importance on the management of local environments: his approach was to secure a cellular composition to a town's structure by means of a hierarchical road pattern of primary, secondary and distributory roads which would give order to traffic circulation and which would create environmental areas where traffic volumes could be kept to acceptable levels. The principle of traffic management for environmental areas is still accepted, though the costs of radically re-ordering urban form in this way have proved too great to do much in this direction. However, a general acceptance of traffic restraint in the interests of a liveable environment has entered deeply into planning attitudes.

The focus of attention has shifted to national road policy and particularly to the building of motorways; here, public opposition has reached new heights through a variety of protest groups in respect of such epic battles as the M16 through Epping Forest, the M25 (Ripley Inquiry) and the Aire Valley, Winchester and Archway Road Inquiries. The issue is even more important than simply a change in values and attitudes; it is significant for the planning inquiry system and the ways in which public policy is made, debated and declared; questions which will be considered more broadly in the next chapter. John Tyme writes:

First, that public inquiries into road and motorway proposals are a denial of law and justice in that persons whose property and livelihood are affected by them are denied the essential information by which alone they can object to them according to their rights under the Acts. Second, that the road and motorway proposals themselves, with all the immense expenditure involved in them and with all their implications in terms of land use planning and economic development, are entirely without Parliamentary approval. And finally that this country does not have a Department of Transport, but a Department of Highways, which possesses the power to make policy decisions on railways and waterways and, furthermore, which exercises this power not in the national interest, but in the interests of one industrial/financial lobby – in short, that it constitutes a corruption of government and thus a major threat to our democracy.[45]

He proceeds to make two major proposals. First, a Transport Directorate should be set up, composed of the Department of Transport and Environment, road, rail and water boards and local authorities, charged with the preparation of a national transport policy and programme. Second, there should be a Parliamentary Select Committee on Transport. These innovations would not only ensure that national policy would be subject to public scrutiny, but also that the Secretary of State and his officials were accountable to Parliament.

Thus the questions of road traffic and transportation are strongly linked with town planning, its aims, its methods and its relationship with political and popular attitudes. In any given city the disposition of land uses, the road network and forms of transport contribute much to the function and convenience of that city. There are choices to be made between road and rail and between forms of road layout. Moreover, these choices cannot be made simply on the basis of a calculation as to cost effectiveness; the choices are in fact highly political because the consequences have various effects on different population groups.

British city transport strategies, typified in London but broadly reflected elsewhere, have been based on the principle of traffic limitation. Private transport has been discouraged, particularly in central areas, because of the heavy social cost of extensive investment in environmental engineering to counteract unacceptable levels of noise, pollution and disturbance. Public transport, both road and rail, has been favoured and land uses are planned to concentrate activities and travel into corridors, well served by the public sector. These strategies have permitted the maintenance of a strong, commercial city centre; elsewhere, sector, suburban and neighbourhood centres are developed as functional hierarchies. But matters are different elsewhere in the world, as Michael Thomson has recently shown.[46] Los Angeles is a city devoted to full motorisation, and this has necessitated the abandonment of the traditional form of city with its dominant commercial and business core. Elsewhere, cities may have had an important nineteenth century centre and there will be strong vested interests in its survival. Nonetheless there will also be forces for decentralisation, and so compromises have to be reached. Sometimes, an appropriate transport system will permit the continuing dominance of the city centre (as in Paris); in other cases the extent of private motorisation will weaken the centre (as in Melbourne). The observation to be made is that forms of transportation, like any other form of planning, have to be the subject of choices, and these cannot be scientifically determined.

Conservation and environmentalism

During the last ten to fifteen years, British town and country planning has been faced increasingly with a set of issues concerned broadly with ecology, natural resources and conservation of the environment. It has been ill–prepared to deal with these issues, and neither the statutory planning framework of post-war legislation nor the procedures for the hearing of the public inquiries has been of very much help.

In the 1940s, conventional wisdom (as enshrined in the Scott Committee *Report on Land Utilisation in Rural Areas*. (1942), held that the appearance and land quality of the British countryside would be protected and maintained by means of a combination of healthy agriculture and land–use control. In fact technological innovations such as mechanisation and the greater use of chemical fertilizers, themselves important bases of productive agriculture, wrought great changes in landscape appearance. Furthermore, control of land use largely exempted agriculture and forestry and proved too blunt an instrument to deal adequately with local, sensitive issues of countryside change. From the late 1960s onwards the long–standing issues which had formed the subject field of countryside planning (protection from urban development, recreation planning and the problems of the rural commuter and traditional villages) began to be overtaken by new questions relating to environmental protection and management (a new consciousness about non-renewal resources and the conservation of the land-scape). Max Nicholson's *The Environmental Revolution* (1970), Barbara Ward's *The Home of Man* (1976) and Habitat, the United Nations Conference on Human Settlements held in Vancouver in 1976, typified a new recognition of man's interdependence with nature in a rapidly changing world. Environmental misuse on an international scale caused alarm and in Britain the planning system faced new questions for which the past gave little guidance.

An important shift in attitudes can be detected during the 1970s. O'Riordan has described the change in environmentalist ideology from 'technocentrism' to 'ecocentrism'.[47] On one extreme wing there are (or have been) the 'cornucopians' holding to the view that man can always find a way out of difficulties, ingenuity will overcome impediments, and that scientific and technological expertise will provide the way forward for continuing economic growth and the improvement of our living conditions. Still technocratic, but adopting a somewhat modified position, are the 'environmental managers' who subscribe to the belief that economic growth and resource exploitation can continue, but subject to certain conditions of minimum standards and compensation for disturbance or injurious affection. In the other wing we have first of all the 'self-reliance soft technologists'. They would lack faith in modern large scale technology, preferring to emphasize smallness of scale and community identity in settlement, work and leisure. Beyond this position the 'deep ecologists' would stress ecological laws and the intrinsic importance of nature for the humanity of man, and maintain the right of endangered species or unique landscapes to remain unmolested.

Within these four positions, environmentalism has shifted from the previously held ground of the cornucopians and has come to rest broadly in the area of the environmental managers. However, there is a vigorous minority view which has an ecocentric mode of thought, characterised by a passionate idealism for a radical transformation of values and social organisation. The scene is therefore somewhat confused and British town planning has found it hard to accommodate the various ideas. Some very important issues have been raised; the mining of copper in the Snowdonia National Park by Rio Tinto-Zinc; the exploitation of the Bedfordshire brickfield and aluminium smelting on Anglesey;[48] Scottish oil; the Selby coalfield; the mining potential of the Vale of Belvoir; the loss of moorland on Exmoor and North Yorkshire; the drainage of marshlands; and flooding of reservoirs – to name but a few.

Perhaps the one single issue which has drawn more attention than any other, and which has illustrated the weaknesses of Britain's planning system, is the application by British Nuclear Fuels for permission to build a plant for reprocessing irradiated oxide nuclear fuels at their works at Sellafield, Cumbria. The so-called Windscale Inquiry into the application, which lasted from June to November 1977, resulted in extensive publicity as it performed the function of a debate on nuclear issues. When uranium ore is removed from the reactors it is known as 'spent fuel', and the reprocessing problem is basically that of deciding what to do with it in that condition. It is at that stage highly radio-active and because it produces considerable heat it must be stored for a period to allow the radio-activity and heat to reduce to a level at which it can be handled without undue risk. The issues concerned with the storage and subsequent transportation, and the question as to whether BNFL should take on further reprocessing work for overseas customers attracted considerable attention. In the event, the Inspector recommended outline planning permission, and without delay, having reviewed the conflicting evidence from the possibilities of terrorism, to highly technical questions, and the more conventional planning issues of siting and amenity.

Windscale had a specific and indeed untypical characteristic, but it illustrated the strength and the amorphous nature of the environmental lobby today. There are nationally based associations, local amenity societies and grass roots movements, all forming a loosely-knit pressure group, which is now a political force to be reckoned with. At its worst it can simply encourage an indiscriminate resistance to change; or it can foster the self-interest of an already privileged group while claiming to act for 'national' interests; at its best it can be an important corrective to the imposed values of scientific rationality. The significance for town planning has been described by Howard Newby: 'The debate over environmentalism and the countryside is in reality a deeply political one, revealing issues which are the very stuff of politics: distributional justice; individual freedom versus a planned allocation of resources; the impact of science and technology on society; the defence of private property rights; the expansion of individual choice and the satisfaction of social needs.'[49]

The planning experience of the last three decades has been a strange one. Despite high hopes and a belief in a comprehensive approach to land-use control, the situation now is marked by a collapse of confidence, and any notion of integrated economic, social and land planning is extraordinarily elusive. The scientific bases of planning have proved imperfect and there is now greater reliance on guidance offered by values and preferences. Planning has become weak rather than strong, but paradoxically now demonstrates a greater explicitness of political purpose than ever before. It is also remarkable that in the post-war period, more and more demands for planning have led to sharper and sharper denunciations of its alleged failures. Over the last ten years it has become almost obligatory in planning literature to give evidence of failure, by the profession and by the central and local State. Public policy with regard to community and environmental affairs has been attacked on a broad front. Local authority housing provision has not overcome social and spatial inequalities. Land-use policies aimed at decentralisation and dispersal have helped to cause inner-city problems. The slowness of planning machinery has caused urban blight and decay. Land price inflation has not been stopped; indeed it may have accelerated due to green belt restrictions. Transport policies have not halted environmental damage. The regional problem continues; we are still 'two nations'. And where are our beautiful cities?

Town planning then is not what it was, its performance is under the sharpest of public scrutiny, and there is confusion as to its purpose. Donald Denman writes: 'We have come to the point where planning the use of resources in land from the national angle has become so demanding of time and money in both the public and private sectors as to call in question the benefits and to ask whether they are not far outweighed by the burdens. And there is a graver malady. We seem to have lost all knowledge of why we plan the use of land.'[50] He concludes that 'land use planning in the UK has become a process without a purpose'. Is this so? Has post-war planning run into the sand? Can relations between the political, bureaucratic and community systems be improved to give more acceptable results? To answer these questions it is necessary to look at the important issues before planning today.

Chapter six
TODAY'S POLITICAL QUESTIONS

It may be argued that whatever is wrong with town planning today and whatever are its limitations and imperfections, the questions to be asked of it are political rather than professional or technical, and, by the same token, political answers are required. Its aims, objectives, methods and institutional framework need to be assessed from a political perspective.

A GENERAL ASSESSMENT

It is argued that town planning has been given the political authority to be one of the important influences to shape our 20th century environment. Land use control, an instrument designed to establish the right use of land, has helped to fashion the urban and regional map of Britain. In particular, British cities have been reconstructed and enlarged over the last 35 years to publicly approved schema, while countryside areas have been protected from urban development. From a primacy of concern with suburban layouts 70 years ago there is now scarcely any aspect of our environment with which town planning is not involved: the regional question, landscape preservation, National Parks, recreation and tourism, planning for natural resources, transport and transportation, conservation and the energy question, housing and social policy, quality of life, employment and economic strategies. Town planning has become an essential ingredient of contemporary public policy, playing a part in the advances of social welfare programmes and contributing to the provision of an environment based on precepts of amenity, convenience and health. What began as an elitist form of urban design has become welded into democratic forms of environmental and community management. Major social objectives such as lower density, the maintenance and preservation of open land and the separation of town from country have been powerfully bolstered by political authority. Furthermore, the precepts of ideal cities and social reconstruction have rarely been far from the political surface.

But neither politicians nor professionals can rest on their laurels. In a fast changing world the qualitative aspects of life have become more important than quantitative gains, and because town planning deals constantly with value judgements rather than fixed scientific norms, public opinion has recorded some unpredictable reactions to planning achievements. An urban motorway or a regional highway may be seen as impressive technological progress one decade, an environmental nuisance the next. Similarly a particular housing design can at first be thought innovative (high rise for example) but later a sociological disaster. In the wider environmental field a fast breeder nuclear reactor may be regarded first as a major scientific contribution to the energy crisis, but subsequently attacked as an ecological hazard. Public preferences have become more and more fickle in an age of affluence, and today town planning is beset with real flash points in clashes of social values.

In the mid 1940s through to the mid 1950s planned change was widely held to represent an improvement in our national lives; professionals had the skills, politicians gave the authority, and the community largely endorsed or acquiesced. Today the popular judgement has changed: what is new is not necessarily better than the old. Discontent with the results of our environmental achievements has bred a scepticism against the claims of change. Uncertainty about the future has replaced the wartime confidence in ability to achieve planned solutions. New hopes are discarded almost before they are adequately tested; and planning is regarded as simply maverick in its method and application, inadequately rooted in theory and empirical evidence. Model building and application of quantitative method were seen as important keys to rational planning 15 years ago; we are now in danger of rejecting scientific methods as over-hastily as they were adopted. At the same time democratised processes through public participation were held to bring novel benefits of public opinion to planning decisions. Now it is fashionable to deride participation as unthinkingly as it was popular to adopt it.

The fact is that adaptability and change is inherent in town planning because of its strong political context. Planning is both culture and time bound. Town planning ideas and practice were different in 1980 from, say, 1930 and will be different again in 2030. In the search for amenity, convenience and order in our environment there will be many ways forward: town planning is grounded in socio-economic, cultural and political contexts; its legitimacy springs from society, and is fixed in political and institutional frameworks. Hence town planning is different in the USA from that in Britain, and different again from the USSR. There may be many ayotollahs but no one Koran in town planning; there are re-current threads of principle but what may be regarded as 'good planning' changes over time and between cultures. Town planning is always at the centre of a moving scene, revolving round the core concerns of environmental management and the right use of land. Town planning is therefore not an exact science; it is much more an art in which there are changing responses to periodic expressions of social values. This emphasises the political context; town planning can never be finally described or defined in terms of right or wrong, because its determinants are not scientific norms but cultural and societal preferences, mediated through the exercise of political au-thority.

These observations stress what has been illustrated throughout this book: the indissoluble bonds between the professional skills of town planning and the political process. Environmental and related community problems have origins which at least in part are social; policies have also social consequences. Town planning has become part of the community's distribution of resources, rewards and opportunities, and is thereby concerned with the politics of decision making – the making of decisions on behalf of others in the institu-tional framework of governance.

There have been professionals and politicians this century who have thought it possible that we might harness social reconstruction to the creation of magnificent new cities. This was certainly articu-lated in the aftermath of World War II. How wrong they have been! A harmonious post-war society has not replaced the earlier targets of disorder and conflict; social problems have not been solved by the prolific extension of human knowledge; and creative design has been stifled by the democratic hand which called it forth. Both planning and politics might now be criticised for run-ning out of ideas; what was seen as the bow wave of progress may now be seen as the wash of the past.

In defence, neither the town planner nor the politician are all-powerful and they can only be agents amongst many in a social democracy. Cities for example are extraordinarily complex and insti-tutions of governance have neither the capacity to understand nor the political will to respond to the variety exhibited in the community or the environment. Town planning in the past has imposed an unreal simplicity on cities, as perhaps illustrated by Abercrombie's Greater London Plan. No longer can this be the case, because town planning today deals with the incrementalism of *process*, rather than the static concerns of *ends*. The blueprint master plan has been replaced by the control of complex systems over time. The political expectations of town planning have irrevocably changed.

As a consequence, a number of criticisms of town planning have appeared in recent years.[1] In the first place the planning system has failed to produce what it promised. It has proved strong with regard to issues that are relatively unimportant, and weak and ineffective in dealing with things that matter much more, such as major locational or distribution questions which might lead to personal satisfactions in jobs, housing and life chances. (To be fair, however, 'planning' is often a synonym for the whole bureaucratic system for housing, education and the social services, and town planning gets blamed for defects in wider social welfare arrangements). It is argued that town planning has failed to create truly satisfying, physical environments and the whole operation of plan making with its mystique is alleged to have become distant from the people. It has failed to be 'positive' in the sense of creative innovation, and has been 'negative', in that it has caused unnecessary restriction. It has on occasions been regressive, and has contributed to difficulties. Finally, in spite of high hopes the planning system has failed to coordinate the plans of other public services: town planning is imperfectly related to other spheres of State policy and activity, either at local and central levels. It has proved difficult to achieve coordinated activity to any meaningful extent; there has been some coordination with regard to the arrangement of land uses, but financial and operational coordination has been weak. Frequent criticism is that large tracts of land have been left vacant (and sometimes derelict in inner city areas) for many years, and services and facilities have not been provided when required.

Secondly, the 'failure to produce' argument is accompanied by the further criticism that town planning is too slow and demanding of manpower. Inevitably the existence of a planning system which involves the preparation and approval of public plans, and the application to a local authority for permission to build or develop land, introduces extra stages in the process of development which require time and manpower; the criticism is that these requirements have become excessive. In addition to this, arrangements for the preparation and usefulness of Structure Plans and Local Plans have come under fire, while the arbitrary nature of decision making has been a constant criticism.

Third, town planning has proved to be a source of public confrontation and dispute; it is alleged to have contributed to delays, thereby weakening the status and reputation of local government and central government. (To be fair, town planning will, of course, always be associated with disputes because of its political character, whereby benefits are bestowed on some to the disadvantage of others.) The difficulty is that the machinery for resolving disputes is cumbersome and imperfect. The public inquiry arrangements are ponderous, and some of the wider environmental questions have been quite inadequately explored to public satisfaction. There is further dispute between tiers of government, particularly between counties and districts. Finally, the arrangements for public participation, designed to resolve or defuse public controversy, may be awkwardly handled by local authorities, and the results frankly disappointing.

These are the serious defects of town planning today, and they derive from political factors as much as from professional and technical factors. The planning process needs to be more effective, more expeditious, and more commanding of public respect. It is not going to be easy to achieve these aims quickly, particularly at a time when local politics are volatile and any consensus for reform is largely absent. The Royal Institute of Public Administration and the Policy Studies Institute have jointly reported a more assertive style in local politics today with ideology from both Right and Left playing a greater part in the development of policy.[2] Party disputes over the allocation of resources have been sharpened in the climate of limited or nil economic growth. Wildly changing electoral results have led to rapid switches in political control, and throughout the local authority world, professional planners point to the increasingly political nature of local affairs.

One difficulty is that the role of the local government officer lacks definition; professional and managerial responsibilities merge; and administration slides into policy. Local government too is ambiguous; local authorities draw legal and constitutional authority from statute, but political authority from their local electorate. In these circumstances the relationships between local government officers and elected members can pose serious difficulties. In the past, there could be reliance on the Town Clerk, the key officer responsible for the smooth administration of his authority who advised the Council on the issues before them. More recently the

Chief Executive, a kind of general manager, has not had an easy role to follow, in part at least because of the considerable differences that exist between the practice of public and private management. A further difficulty for the local government officer occurs when his role is equated to that of civil servant to Minister, the obligation being that political neutrality accompanies loyalty to the Committee Chairman and administration of the day. All these problems have been exposed with the growing influence of party politics in local government, especially now that effective power in most local authorities rests today with the party group. The planner finds himself increasingly in the position of broker between politics and administration, with influence but without power.

This background of controversy has so far put a smokescreen over the important questions relating to town planning which are of significance to both professionals and politicians alike. It is timely that they should be considered:

1 *How much* planning is now thought desirable? In view of the failures of the public sector will the importance previously attached to collective demands now reside with private preferences? What are the likely socio-political attitudes and postures towards town planning over the next quarter of a century? Is the current 'retreat from government' a short term hiccup or a long term trend?

2 *What forms* of planning can we best arrange? Will it be possible to devise comprehensive planning strategies and programmes? The necessary elements include public involvement and partnership, forms of administrative coordination and an effective means of reconciling conflict: our performance so far has been relatively poor – are we deluding ourselves if we say we can improve our showing?

3 *What levels* of planning will be thought desirable? We might speculate that we need tiers of devolved government with more central direction in some areas but less in others. Clear and unambiguous tiers at neighbourhood, local authority and regional levels seem to be needed. Are we able to reduce the present conflict both within local government and between central and local government: limitations which are so damaging to effective town planning?

4 *What focus* for planning? Land-use control was once seen as the focus in the belief that it represented a coordinating function; town planning was therefore a technical exercise, demanding professional skills. 'Labels' are very convenient for both pro-

fessionals and politicians, but problems change, and sometimes new problems go unchallenged because of an inability to identify them. Can our planning be more policy orientated, and move on from its apolitical origins? Is not the true focus of town planning urban (and rural and regional) management?

HOW MUCH PLANNING?

Town planning today has to be seen in the general context of the extension of State enterprise over the last 150 years. The objectives have been to tackle the problems thrown up in the economic, social and technological transformations of that period, and to provide the amenities and community rewards for an increasingly prosperous society, which the capitalist order, unaided, could not be relied upon to provide. In this period, greater and greater has become the role of the State, narrower and narrower have been the opportunities for individual enterprise.

In Britain, and throughout the social democracies of Western Europe, there has developed since the Second World War, a compromise between central planning on the one hand, and a reliance on market forces on the other. The context of British town planning over the last thirty five years has been the political oscillations between these two poles. The question throughout has been how far Government action could secure land and environmental planning results qualitatively different from those of the operation of the free market. The market in fact stands in rival opposition to the machinery of central planning, and support for or distrust of it has provided an instinctive basis for the attitudes of the Labour and Conservative Parties. The ideological spectrum is blurred, however, as we have seen, because cutting across party lines is a middle-class tradition of benevolent social concern. Nonetheless there is an important distinction, and in matters relating to property and land values town planning has a very definite political perspective.

Town planning and planning generally have come under sharp scrutiny from both the Left and Right. Questions are being asked again as to the role of the State in post-industrial society. To what extent do private markets need correction? How large should public expenditure be and what areas should it underpin? How vital is a strong public sector? Is there a middle way, between two extremes, through the wise management of capitalism? What about personal freedoms – is individualism the best safeguard? Can the private market deal with the uncertainty of the future better than the machinery of a central authority? The inter–war period suggested that free markets do not work: do the same assumptions still apply? When and where does the State intervene? (As Alan Budd remarks: 'It is true that the United States have been notoriously poor in providing urban amenities. It does seem absurd that lavatory paper can be provided in every colour but that it is apparently impossible to provide an efficient or even a safe public transport system.'[3] Is not public sector intervention important, not only to secure efficiency but equity? How far is it possible to have State planning and still preserve the maximum possible freedom of choice for individuals? Labour's rejection of socialism, post war, in favour of welfare capitalism has put strains on some traditional town planning objectives, such as the replacement of the anarchy of private competition by ordered land planning under public control: is this form of modified town planning an effective compromise?

From the Right, arguments have been advanced which have advocated a substantial retreat from bureaucracy at all levels. In previous chapters it has been shown that the views of Heseltine and Joseph point to a new political climate in this respect. Their arguments have stressed that unnecessary state control of our community affairs is wrong in principle and merely serves to weaken the capacity of the individual to enhance his own life chances. They point to the fact that the actual post-war fruits of State control have often been unpalatable and that the results have not always been in the interests of those most affected. They dismiss the idea that town planning is always 'progressive', maintaining that in fact it can be regressive, contributing to a new set of problems. (The emergence of the inner-city problem, for example, where redevelopment programmes accelerated economic decline and a population flight, is held as an example.) The insensitivies of planning bureaucracies are given as unwelcome manifestations of state power, while its inefficiencies are compared to the more attractive features of adaptive private market intelligence.

Consequently it has been reasserted that certain private markets can be effectively self regulating, without the need for much state supervision or guidance. 'Planning free zones' have therefore been advocated, favouring private markets in health, housing, education, welfare and land. The argument is that the way forward is to let the State do those things it does well, and elsewhere to permit other arrangements whereby a collective set of individual actions can at best be loosely fettered.

From the Left have come a variety of criticism, broadly suspicious of the power of the State. The Marxist would argue that State involvement in town planning, to secure objectives in spatial organisation and environmental management, simply expresses the combined interests of the dominant classes. Manuel Castells, for example, in the context of a French case study of the Dunkerque Region, has written:

Plans stamp all individual schemes with a double character: on the one hand, they come to be seen as 'reasonable', rational technical solutions to the problems posed and, on the other, they appear to bring about a convergence of the various social groups and urban functions. Town planning comes to embody social neutrality, by expressing the general interests of the community, in addition to its advantage of technical neutrality. It is for this reason that planning is a privileged instrument for the ideological embodiment of the interests of classes, fractions and groups; it increases opportunities for social integration to the maximum, a prime function of dominant ideology.[4]

The same sort of analysis comes from James Simmie's recent study of development planning and development control in Oxford.[5] In tracing the influence of the organisations and groups involved in determining the content of the City Development Plan, Simmie maintains that his evidence points to the importance of the major landowning, industrial and commercial organisations in setting the objectives of the Plan. These same organisations have successfully organised beneficial property rights and minimised the costs of acquisition of land and buildings. On the other hand, other organisations like trade unions and the Labour Party have secured improvements, particularly for skilled workers, in services such as housing and education, and in provision of amenity facilities. Conversely, unorganised groups, who do not have their interests effectively represented in the corporate power structure, come off badly, bearing regressive costs.

An even sharper observation comes from a study of planning in Lambeth: the State in capitalism is an instrument of class domination with the bourgeoisie, the dominant class who own capital, employ workers, and hold political sway. Cynthia Cockburn argues that the characteristic function of the State is repression: 'its main role is to keep the working class in its place and to set things up, with forceful sanctions, in such a way that capital itself, business interests as a whole, normally survive and prosper.'[6] Local government in which town planning plays such a significant part, is a key part of the State in capitalist society, and her conclusions on its role and performance do not make easy reading for the older professionals today, brought up to believe that they were operating an apolitical system. She writes:

> We have been taught to think of local government as a kind of humane official charity, a service that looks after us 'from the cradle to the grave', protects us from the misfortunes of life, hardships such as poverty and homelessness that fall on us by fate – or are perhaps even our own fault. If the town hall doesn't seem to work in our interest we put it down to 'inefficiency' or 'red tape'. It is by no means obvious that a local council is part of a structure which as a whole and in the long term has other interests to serve than our own.

But Cockburn believes those interests to be different – what a contrast to Chamberlain's and Simon's views on local government (see p. 62–3).

In recent years Marxist theories of capitalist development, which integrate economic, political and ideological factors in the analysis of society, have had a strong influence on analysis of the political economy of space. Concepts of, and attitudes towards, town planning have inevitably been affected. The argument has been advanced that the State has a key role in enforcing the dominance of the ruling class and the subordination of the working class. State power therefore exists to ensure the continuance of the capitalist system.

It can be readily acknowledged that what happens in the name of town planning reflects the interests of those who wield power and influence. It is not obvious, however, that State power is dominant and that we can 'explain' town planning in terms of conflict between class interests. Explanations of town planning are much more difficult; theoretical abstractions offer one level of explanation, but more penetrating analysis suggests that reality is much more muddied. The interplay, in Britain at least, of the actors concerned in the planning process, and all the adjustments to power structures, influence and expressions of preferred values, makes the operation of planning take place in a complex system of checks and balances. For example, between the population and the capitalist economy is a central group of mediators, the 'managers' who occupy a crucial role in generating and maintaining the ideology of the Welfare State. Pahl, in writing on 'urban managerialism', has claimed that urban managers are 'central to the urban problematic'.[7]

The complexity is confirmed by McKay and Cox, who in their analysis of national urban policy since 1945, assert that 'theories which deny any independent role for the State in urban society are oversimplifications' and that Marxist claims that all State actions necessarily serve the interests of capital 'can be quickly dismissed'.[8] They point to many policies which derive much more from party ideology and competition, and administrative complexities, than from links between policies and the interests of capital. On the other hand, it is only fair to point out that another recent observer of urban planning in a capitalist society, Gwyneth Kirk, argues that 'a Marxist perspective has the most to offer for an understanding of the land use planning system, compared to the other perspectives considered, though it is not without its problems.'[9] My own view of the course of town planning this century, both pre−war and post−war, is that while there have been some very obvious beneficiaries (the middle and upper income suburbanite or the land and property speculator for example) there can be no simple conclusion that the interests of class and capital have directed and manipulated the planning system for their overriding advantage. Indeed, there seems to be far more evidence to suggest positively no such consistent basis to the making of town planning policy. Careful empirical work indicates that it is extremely implausible to offer explanations of particular planning events or policies which root them conclusively in the conflict between the forces of class and capital. The enforced superimposition of the simple on the complex is just not convincing.

At the risk of compressing a voluminous literature of the last ten years or so, it may be said that the Marxist view is that there are no urban or regional questions as such; they are only general descriptive features of a wider social system – the capitalist use of land and the exploitative character of its social organisation. The contemporary problems of the city are therefore seen in terms of the territorial structure of late capitalism, itself in crisis: increasing social disintegration, high unemployment, 'margination' of population groups such as the young, old, women and ethnic minorities, fiscal crises, decreasing efficiency of public services, and increasingly uneven regional development. It is held that whereas contemporary capitalist societies have proved able to survive for a long time on welfare ideologies, they have proved unable to guarantee social justice and to provide lasting solutions to the distribution of wealth and opportunity. This argument maintains that capitalism forces the working class to pay as many economic and social costs as possible. There are spatial implications to this, as Mingione, a marxist sociologist, explains:

... the working class will be asked to bear increasingly longer, unpaid commuting times, and to accept increases in income taxes to pay for the re-establishment of the ecological equilibrium damaged by industrial development. It will have to tolerate environmentally dangerous but capitalistically convenient settlements, be obliged to move into suburban segregated areas which happen to be more expensive and less comfortable than the central ones, and so on.[10]

The difficulty is that the 'working class' has become a term almost devoid of meaning, and in Britain at least we suspect that the spatial structure of our cities has not been determined in quite the simplistic way suggested above.

What will be the future position of the public sector and how will it affect town planning? On the one hand it seems that the present 'retreat from government' will significantly gather pace. At the present time it is expressed in opposition to rates and taxes, the over-abundance of civil servants and local government officers, and unwelcome constraints on private freedoms. In the future the argument would be that public services will sharply decline to such an extent that public sector environmental planning will become atrophied. The statutory base for planning work would be systematically withdrawn; public support for planning would decline and professional morale collapse. Town planning would relapse into moral exhortation and real achievements would be limited to experiments of an early twentieth century kind.

On the other hand there is a contrary speculation, that the case for limiting public sector planning, so strongly articulated at the present time, may in fact turn out to be little more than a temporary hiatus in a longer term canvas that sees continuing political support in Britain for social and economic goals. This would suggest little long-term change in the social and economic involvement by the State in community affairs. There may be marginal shifts in what is or what is not seen as better undertaken by individual action or private markets, but overall, centrally directed systems would be strongly represented. There would be conscious attempts to organise space, to distribute resources, to adjudicate amongst competing claims, and to deal with problems private markets cannot settle (such as unemployment, social casualties, energy, and food supply).

Even given this maintenance of a strong public sector, however, there would still be alternative futures which would significantly affect town planning. It might be that sustained pressure for community decisions to be made at the lowest possible levels of government would prevail, leaving higher echelons to coordination and policy making. Town planning practice would therefore be much concerned with local planning. Area management schemes would develop at the local level; district councils would be strong, parish councils would develop; health services might return to being the responsibility of local authority. Strategic planning at a wider geographic scale would be removed from this level of government.

Another possible future would be the very antithesis of this. Disillusionment with local government might lead to such growth in central control powers that new functional agencies would be created to take over major activities of local government. New forms of Urban Development Corporations, much more extensive in scale and number than those presently proposed, would be set up, and these would have the effect of reducing local government to a range of limited service functions.

Or Britain might move towards a federal structure. If this came about, town planning would become an activity essentially within a system of regionally elected governments. A system of proportional representation would encourage the activities of the smaller political parties, particularly in marginal areas, and there would be a resurgence of regionalism. Local authorities would have a regional orientation.

In short, just as there are different economic, social and technological futures, there are also different institutional futures.[11] Town planning for the rest of this century and into the twenty–first century will be shaped accordingly. 'How much planning' depends on the extent to which society will be prepared to ask the State to deal with community and environmental problems, rather than ask other agencies, institutions or markets. A feature of post-war Britain has been the almost unwavering support given to State involvement in many fields. An equal feature is the very considerable criticism of the results of that State involvement. The weight of that criticism may lead to a profound reluctance to repose any more confidence in the State to act effectively in environmental, economic, social and community affairs. If so, town planning would be one of those areas to experience significant consequences.

FORMS OF PLANNING

We are here concerned with two matters: planning instruments and involvement with the public. The first is a technical question relating to the nature of the plans drawn up at various levels of government, to which there will be further reference in the next chapter. The larger issue is distinctly political in nature and concerns the means of reconciling opposing views in a sensitive, speedy and effective way. The various factors involved require some elaboration.

It is now a prerequisite throughout the Western social democracies that in town planning matters citizens be provided with opportunities of direct involvement in decisions that substantially affect their lives. Britain's record in holding public hearings, inquiries, and examinations on town planning questions that affect private rights and public interest this century is an honourable one. But since the late 1960s, new efforts have been put into more effective public participation, rather than inquiries into objections, following the recommendations of the Skeffington Report, *People and Planning* (1969).[12]

The Committee on Public Participation in Planning was appointed in 1968 by the Minister of Housing and Local Government (MHLG), (Anthony Greenwood) and the Secretaries of State for Scotland and Wales (William Ross and George Thomas) 'to consider and report on the best methods, including publicity, of securing the participation of the public at the formative stage in the making of development plans for their area.' The chairman was Arthur Skeffington, Joint Parliamentary Secretary at MHLG; his Committee, rather large with twenty-five members, included a clutch of planners and others active in local government and public service. As the terms of reference required, the Committee's main task was to suggest practical ways in which local planning authorities could best implement the new Town and Country Planning Act (1968), but they went on to examine the broad context in which their recommendations were made.

Skeffington recognised the growing demand for more opportunity to contribute to public policies which affected the community, not just at election time but continuously as proposals were being formulated and later implemented. The Committee's starting point that 'People should be able to say what kind of community they want and how it should develop: and should be able to do so in a way that is positive and first-hand. It matters to us all that we should know that we can influence the shape of our community so that the towns and villages in which we live, work, learn and relax may reflect our best aspirations.' (para 8) There were wider advantages also to be gained: 'As well as giving the individual the chance of saying how his town or village should develop, participation also offers him the opportunity of serving the community and thereby becoming involved in its life, contributing to its well-being and enriching its relationships.' (para 9)

The objective was clear: to establish and maintain a better understanding between the public and the planning authority. The suggested ways forward included community education in planning matters, improved access to information, statutory rights of consultation, openness of planning and local government to the press, and closer links between physical planning and social welfare work. The Committee recommended that local planning authorities should consider convening meetings for the purpose of setting up community forums which would provide local organisations with the opportunity of discussing collectively planning and related issues of importance to the area. The appointment of community development officers would help in the process of stimulating discussion and communicating information to the people and returning their views to the authority.

Today, *People and Planning* reads rather naively. Perhaps that is a measure of the developments and changes in attitudes that have taken place over the last ten years. There can be no doubting Skeffington's honest hopes: 'We want the paper of the plans to come to life; and to come to life in a way that people want.' The potential of the partnership offered by the Town and Country Planning Act (1968) could be realised, for the benefit of both the planner and the planned. But the way forward was in the context of a consensus society, with very little understanding of the complexities of decision making and the exercise of political power in community affairs. In fact consensus was not a characteristic of the 1970s and there was to be no easy rapprochement of views amongst the community groups and between them and public authorities.

But yet in many ways Skeffington hit the right note. Planning was changing, new methods were being adopted, and new power structures were evolving. In spite of all the complexities of the statutory planning process (which participation and all that it implied seemed to further encumber), and in spite, too, of the extra cost and delays for local government (which extensive and continuing consultation procedures undoubtedly produced), the recognition that government was not the sole arbiter of choice in forms of community development, but that groups in the community had greater rights of self expression, was an important marker in social politics. Skeffington was in no way radical; he advocated no change in the system. Final authority still resided unambiguously in elected local government, but an important gate had been opened for experimentation in the conduct of British planning. By implication, the democratisation of planning made way for a period when certainty gave way to uncertainty, and when the articulation of both individual views and collective aspirations and demands could legitimately challenge the established system.

New problems have demanded, and still demand, new measures. Greater awareness of social and environmental questions prompted a demand for wider public engagement in their resolution, particularly where local authorities and central government had appeared out of step with popular wishes. The public sector's business had expanded considerably, as we have seen, and the steady inclusion of larger numbers of technical 'experts' to resolve environmental problems threatened to dilute or override political judgements. The dilemma became increasingly one of ensuring how citizens could influence their own future in a world of increasing complexity, ruled by bureaucracies and large corporations. One result was, as has been shown, the emergence of action or protest groups, aiming to influence or stop decisions relating to the construction of such developments as motorways, airfields, and nuclear power stations. The crucial problem for town planning and its machinery now is to resolve such conflicts within the framework of Britain's system of representative democracy.

This aspect of town planning has caused great difficulties for professionals and politicians alike, largely due to the uncertainty surrounding the issues. It is only with some hindsight that we are able to see the position at all clearly; the relative simplicity and naivety of Skeffington may be excused. At the heart of the matter, in our public stances (and this affects town planning as much as anything) we lack conviction as to what is right or wrong. Concensus has broken down; there is less and less agreement as to what is right, and the issues are increasingly resolved through conflict. Furthermore, a former reliance on professional judgement of complicated issues is now much weaker. Neither are experts necessarily to be trusted, and whole subject fields previously belonging to professionals have been usurped by individuals who, confused by scientific assertions, claim to be their own best experts.

These then are the contemporary issues relating to public participation. Inherited methods of solving problems have proved inadequate. Planning failures by local authorities have led to a rejection of their sole right to make decisions. Underlying this, has been a general fear of people losing control over the direction of their lives, as the effectiveness of representative democracy has become more and more doubtful.

Town planning in the past has sought to escape from politics. It has preferred to be apolitical, standing aloof as paternalist or technocratic, but this is no longer possible or indeed desirable. In developments over the last ten years or so we can observe some of the success of the new kinds of involvement. The Town and Country Planning Act (1968), obliged local authorities in the preparation of their Structure Plans and Local Plans to consult the population concerned. We can now affirm that local opinion is a valuable contribution to decision taking, and that laymen often have insights to compare with the views of experts. Furthermore, it may be conceded that the facility of personal involvement is worthy in itself in so far as it gives personal satisfaction and raises community morale. On the other hand, it must be admitted that the exercise of public participation can raise expectations far higher than are often justified, and that in many cases the decisions taken are not qualitatively better. Furthermore, it is a costly exercise, it slows down the process, and there are many issues, particularly those of a complex technical nature, which frankly are beyond the competence of a lay public to decide. Overall we can say that those who get involved in public issues are rarely in any way representative of a wider public, and that the whole process can degenerate into lobbying for special privilege.

Much of the conflict which the town planning process has been obliged to accommodate has come from lobbyists. Pressure groups are nothing new in British politics (as witness the Anti–Corn Law League and the Anti–Slavery Society) but the issues on which they campaign have changed. Moreover, there has been a spectacular growth in their numbers. The picture has changed considerably since Stewart's findings of 1958.[13] The *Guardian Directory of Pressure Groups* lists no less than 350 separate organisations. Recent successes, strongly supported by an informed and concerned middle class include the Consumers' Association (formed in 1956), the Campaign for Nuclear Disarmament (1958) and the Child Poverty Action Group (1965).

The town planning system has thus become embroiled in public inquiries into major development schemes. Some of these have been both long and bitter and all reveal, as with the case studies of the Edinburgh Airport expansion and the London Motorway Plan[14], the present day inadequacies of the British planning system.

Despite the frustration felt by planners with the antics of

environmental preservationists, there are serious issues to be resolved about the conduct of planning inquiries. Democratic safeguards have to be preserved, as John Tyme reminds us.[15] A study of the M3 at Winchester has concluded that trunk road planning procedures were partly responsible for the emergence of public opposition and for the intensity of its activities.

Public debate was stifled by undue ministerial secrecy and, particularly, by the reluctance of the RCU [Road Construction Unit] to provide detailed information about the preferred route or to allow discussion of alternative arguments. Objectors were frustrated also at the Inquiry by the ambiguity concerning the Inspector's competence to consider aspects of the scheme that were not directly related to the published route. The need for the M3 extension to Southampton was not open to debate; nor could alternative strategies, such as a Midlands-Southampton motorway, be seriously discussed. In fact the incremental planning of the road network in the area had predetermined the economics of the alignment for the M3 extension.[16]

Another form of town planning protest comes from the development of community politics. As Peter Hain has observed, the community action movement has signalled the emergence of a new style of political action constituting an alternative to orthodox party politics.[17] In the USA President Johnson's 'War on Poverty' programme encouraged community action, and civil rights organisers turned to community campaigns. In Britain the Home Office's Community Development Programme failed to have this effect. British local government found it impossible to have in the same organisational structure staff whose jobs soon took them into positions whereby they were seen to be working against their own councils. Staff appointed as Community Development Officers found themselves in impossible working relationships where loyalty to a common cause was difficult to maintain. The people recruited were often young, and politically radical; they were soon charged with fermenting tenants' action against their own councils rather than working to a set of assumptions dictated by the local authority. There were undoubtedly instances where these Officers were in fact much needed political irritants injected into an ultra-conservative, tradition-bound authority, but the grit in the machinery proved difficult to absorb with any positive benefit, and the experiments were quickly defused. However, new organisations for community consciousness in areas faced with break up of community life have developed and have come into useful conflict with local councils in drawing up plans. There may well be more development along these lines.

Thus, for a number of reasons, town planning has shed its former image (post-war until the mid 1960s) where professionals and administrators as public officials were the key actors, where politicians were largely acquiescent, and where the public had a muted role. With regard to London, for example, Elkin has expressed his surprise at the extent to which governmental decisions have been made largely by officers, abetted by politicians, with citizens and their spokesmen playing a comparatively limited role.[18] By the end of the 1960s, for the reasons we have described above, the political dimensions of planning became more important as land-use decisions were seen to involve questions of social advantage to particular groups. Public officials found it increasingly difficult to define the public interest in town planning policy and the best ways of achieving it. Since then the situation has shown no signs of clarification and today represents an uneasy, unresolved problem area.

LEVELS OF PLANNING

The State not only defines the limits of town planning through statutory and non-statutory procedures, it also establishes the forms of organisation through which planning policies are developed. In recent years the importance of the structure of local government has been very apparent amongst these organisational forms. Attempts at local government reform, with intended improvements in town planning performance very much at the heart of the matter, have had disappointing results, and town planning has been affected by the surrounding disenchantment.

The Local Government Act (1972) introduced the reform by sweeping away in 1974 (for England and Wales) the old system of counties, county boroughs, and urban and rural district councils, inherited from before the end of the nineteenth century. These gave way to a system of county and county district councils. It also proved convenient in 1974 to introduce new regional water authorities and new health authorities.

Comprehensive local government reform was long overdue. The Attlee Administration resisted the temptation and subsequent Governments relied on a small number of *ad hoc* measures to deal with the worst of the anomolies. Rapidly expanding urban areas, Luton and Solihull, became county boroughs; and in the middle 1960s some rationalisations were made to the local government map with the creation of Teesside and Torbay county boroughs and a new county borough structure for the West Midlands. But Crossman, as

Minister of Housing and Local Government, called a halt to *ad hoc* reform and appointed a Royal Commission in May 1966, under the chairmanship of Lord Redcliffe-Maud. It reported in June 1969.[19]

It is interesting to reflect on the basic faults which the Commission found with local government at that time. It was thought that local government areas did not fit the pattern of life and work, and it was believed that the gap would widen. Fragmentation of boroughs and counties, and the division of town from country, it was argued, had made the proper planning of development and transportation impossible. The division of responsibility between counties and county districts was noted, with county boroughs existing as administrative islands; this situation, led to fragmented services and failed to meet comprehensive needs. Furthermore, many local authorities were too small in size, with an insufficient revenue base to do their work effectively.

These faults led to a number of failings in relationships between local government and the public. The Commission thereupon established important principles which should govern reform, and the logic expressed itself in a preferment for a relatively small number of single tier, unitary authorities. Fifty-eight were proposed, with three metropolitan areas (covering Liverpool, Birmingham and Manchester) in addition, with the key functions of planning, transportation and control over major development.

One of the Commissioners, Derek Senior, published a Memorandum of Dissent[20] based on a fundamental difference of approach. Maud had adopted a principle of organisation and had determined a range of population size for the proposed authorities, but Senior argued that this was in isolation from the geographical context in which local government had to operate. He preferred to start by analysing the facts of social geography and local conditions, and this helped him to determine the appropriate scales of units for groups of related functions. The result was his recommendation for a predominantly two-tier system of local government, with thirty-five directly elected regional authorities and 148 district authorities.

The Wilson Government accepted the principles of the Maud Report in a White Paper of February 1970.[21] But the Conservatives, with Peter Walker as Secretary of State for the Environment, opposed it, and in their White Paper of February 1971[22], reverted to a proposed two-tier structure. Forty-four new county councils were proposed, and six metropolitan counties; as far as town planning was concerned, district councils were also to become planning authorities. In Scotland, where reorganisation took effect in 1975, there are important differences to the English and Welsh two-tier system. In central Scotland the situation is that there are regional and district councils (and Strathclyde with 2.5 million people has nearly half the population of Scotland). Elsewhere on the mainland, the regions are general planning authorities and the districts have no planning functions. In Orkney, Shetland and the Western Isles there are no district councils.

These fundamental changes were accompanied by the removal of three major functions from local government: personal health services, water supply and sewerage disposal. The first was unified under *ad hoc* area health committees and boards, together with the hospitals. The other two became the responsibility of regional water authorities.

Arrangements for local government in London were made separately, as has usually been the case. Over the last century a variety of structures has been followed. In 1855, the Metropolitan Board of Works was established, primarily to tackle the problems of drainage and sewerage. Covering most of the metropolis it did not replace the existing local authorities, and was, in fact, elected by them. The London County Council, a directly elected body, was set up in 1888 and the following year the chaotic jumble of lower tier authorities within the LCC was replaced (except for the City of London) by twenty-eight directly elected metropolitan boroughs. This was the first two-tier local governmental structure in Britain, but it was soon the subject of modification, partly because the LCC did not cover the whole of the built up area of London, so that with territorial expansion the boundaries became less and less suitable. In 1902, the Metropolitan Water Board was established, to be followed in 1908 by the Port of London Authority, and in 1933 by the London Passenger Transport Board. Meanwhile a Royal Commission on London Government was set up in 1921 under the chairmanship of Lord Ullswater; reporting in 1923, it found, rather weakly, that there were no grounds for considering changes in boundaries.

Thirty-five years elapsed before another Royal Commission, this time chaired by Sir Edwin Herbert, was set up to make recommendations on the government of Greater London. There was then a general feeling that reorganisation was timely, though in political circles at least there was great uncertainty as to what was required; in the event a group of academics at the London School of Economics under the leadership of William Robson had significant influence. A new two-tier structure was recommended: a directly elected

GLC embracing the whole metropolis and fifty-two new London borough councils plus an unchanged anachronistic City of London. The GLC was to be given those special services needing a metropolitan scale administration (including planning). Education was split; policy and finance was to be the responsibility of the GLC, while the boroughs would be concerned with day-to-day school management. Government broadly accepted these recommendations, but the area of the GLC was reduced by 140 square miles (the opposition of the surrounding authorities being critical) and the number of boroughs was reduced to thirty-two. Furthermore, education was not split, and the boroughs were given full responsibility; this in turn caused further contention and Government finally brought the thirteen inner boroughs together for educational purposes, so creating the Inner London Education Authority.

Following legislation in 1963, the new GLC system came into operation in 1965. But once again modifications soon followed. The Transport (London) Act (1969) introduced a measure of policy control at metropolitan level; the Water Act (1973) transferred responsibility from the GLC to new water authorities; and the National Health Service Reorganisation Act (1973) transferred the London Ambulance service to new regional health authorities. Continuing uncertainty over roles and functions were reflected in 1977, when the GLC invited Sir Frank Marshall, a former Leader of Leeds City Council and much involved in local government matters, to undertake a review of its role. His report recommended a clarification and strengthening of the metropolitan role. But the issues continue to be politically charged and the concept of 'apt and convenient local government' remains as elusive as ever.

The result of reorganisation has been to bring major changes to local government, substantially different from those proposed by Maud. Controversy has raged since. It has been alleged that relations between counties and their districts are poor, and that work is slow and often duplicated. Large cities resent their district council status; Peter Shore, towards the end of the Callaghan Administration, promised 'organic change' to rectify some anomolies in this field, but the idea fell with the change of government.

In spite of reorganisation therefore, no one can pretend that local government today forms an effective and convenient framework for town planning. There is no regional tier, even though problems manifest themselves at regional scale and demand policies of regional application. At the other end of the scale, the creation of parish councils to represent local views at less than district level, has so far been haphazard and the subject of controversy. The division of responsibilities between counties and districts is unclear (or conveniently alleged to be unclear), particularly with regard to what constitutes 'major development', a county responsibility.

The imperfections are probably worst in the metropolitan areas. The confusion can be seen in the three different systems of metropolitan government in Britain today.[23] London has its Greater London Council and its Boroughs. Glasgow has its Strathclyde Region and Districts. The other English conurbations (including, curiously, South Yorkshire) have the Metropolitan County and County District pattern. There are obviously similarities in these three systems: from the town planning point of view the conurbation authority is responsible for strategic matters and transportation, with the lower tier authority having responsibility for housing, local planning and environmental health. But differences exist with regard to social services, education and consumer protection.

The problems thus centre around confusion, duplication and overlap, compounded by uncertainties as to shared functions, political differences, and animosities, first between districts and counties and then between central and local government generally. Strategic powers are weak and local community groups are poorly organised. The essential political question for the distribution of town planning powers remains: it is to ensure that there is a general compatibility between different population groups and levels of government, and we have not yet achieved this. The ultimate distinction is between a centralised planning machine on the one hand and a system which is more decentralised on the other, permitting participation at lower levels. In short, the key differences are between approaches which are either 'top down' or 'bottom up'. Town planning matters were formerly regarded very much as higher level policy to be prescribed to lower levels; increasingly the trend has been to seek power to determine policy at lower levels. If grass roots democracy is to mean anything at all, the ideal of self—regulating local communities is not to be a sterile dream, and participation in government is not to be captured by unrepresentative pressure groups, then a system whereby appropriate areas of policy reside at community group level, will have to be devised.

THE FOCUS OF TOWN PLANNING

Local government is a key part of the State in our mixed economy society. As Stewart has written:

Our cities and towns can today be regarded in part the creation of the local authority. The local authority may own a third of the property, may have built a third of the buildings; it will have built the road system and allocated the land. It educates the children and deals with the problems of the elderly, handicapped and deprived. It licenses, it approves, it controls, it governs many activities.[24]

Local government has many functions and they are fundamental to government in this country. The provision of facilities (schools, roads, social care, open space, etc.) maintains physical and social infrastructure, essential to the wellbeing and functioning of communities. By establishing different forms of regulation (pertaining to standards of health, licensing and inspection functions, consumer protection, land-use control, and policing) it contributes to a proper ordering of the environment and community affairs. Local government also helps change to occur, both by responding to external pressures, and by initiating change itself.

It should be stressed that local authorities do not do all the work of local government themselves – in many ways the share they do undertake has been getting less and it is not unreasonable to speculate that it could decline further. The fact is that local government presents a very fragmented structure, with many agencies operating at the local level, though outside the local government system. Health, water and transport authorities lie outside; so too do the statutory undertakings which supply gas and electricity. Central government is obviously distinct but does certain things of very great local importance such as running the Post Office, Job Centres and social security offices; it also helps local authorities with rate revenues. There are other national organisations, too, which have a function or an impact at local level: the Housing Corporation, the Commission for Racial Equality and the Sports Council, for example. Local governance therefore is shared by many bodies.

In spite of (or perhaps because of) these observed limitations the past decade has seen considerable interest in local authority management. Towards the end of the 1960s and into the 1970s the concern was to rationalise management structures within local government. Two important commissioned Reports paved the way: *Management of Local Government* (1967)[25] and *The New Local Authorities: Management and Structure* (1972).[26] A powerful movement developed which argued that it was both possible and desirable to plan the affairs of a local authority as a whole. Corporate management became the new gospel which promised an ability to look across functions and so to deal with problems more efficiently and more efffectively. Chief Executives replaced Town Clerks, and management teams and streamlined committee structures replaced a multitude of service-orientated committees. The fact that the high promise has not been achieved and that the idea of rational planning has come under heavy fire from elected members who saw themselves with a lesser role to play in decision taking (both criticisms the subject of much argument) should not detain us here. We have rather to consider the political importance of these recent developments for town planning.

The functioning of local government becomes most significant in towns and cities where effective urban management is vitally important. Britain has a long tradition in this respect: nineteenth-century local government came to terms with appalling urban problems. Just as the Victorians managed their cities, so the requirement remains with us today, and the biggest single organ of governance with this responsibility is local government.

Cities are enormously complex. Town planning has attempted to impose an unreal simplicity on urban phenomena, but simple strategies for complex systems cannot succeed. However, town planning is no longer considered an activity dealing solely with plan making. It used to be concerned primarily with ends, and demonstrated this in the emphasis it placed on plan preparation. But the key to town planning activity today is implementation (process rather than ends) and the incremental management of change. Town planning is then a continuous process, and because of this, a most useful aid to urban management.

The recognition that local government is ultimately concerned with urban (or rural, or regional) management is important to the politics of town planning. Blowers' observation that local politicians sometimes regard planning as 'an esoteric, inpenetrable activity' is no more than town planners may have deserved while they claimed their field to be apolitical and purely technical in nature.[27] But town planning is not that; it is part of the community's distribution of resources, rewards and opportunities, where technical, professional criteria are mediated by political values. It is part of a continuing process of management, bound to no specific time horizons. The proper focus of town planning is not an end in itself as technical exercise, it is part of a wider context; the management of towns, cities and regions.

Chapter seven
FACING THE FUTURE

We are living today in a period of transition. Social authority, once taken as prescribed, is more and more giving way to negotiation, and forms of town planning more suited to earlier decades are naturally subject to stresses and strains. We might argue that town planning in the mixed economy countries has come, not to a cul–de–sac, but to a crossroads. Donnison and Soto, recent commentators on urban development and post-war policy in Britain, have likened the history of British town planning to 'the rise and fall of a loosely knit alliance – the creation over several generations of a reforming coalition of diverse groups with common interests in the orderly management of land, and the recent disintegration of that coalition.'[1] The coalition broke up in the 1960s and since then there has been no recovery of assurance about town planning. There is therefore a clear need to rethink its role, function and preformance.

The directions of land planing, developed in the 1940s, can no longer be pursued unquestioningly. Urban and regional problems are different; the regional metropolitan city has replaced the conurbation; societal aspirations and preferences have changed; community groups demand a greater say in local affairs; and the management of complex urban areas demand new forms of governance. The old approach to town planning, which sought the rational control of space and settlement patterns through scientific norms and criteria is now less relevant; instead we have a flexible planning system of uncertain direction, trying to wrestle with the complexities of economic and social change.

The previous chapter highlighted some of the important questions facing town planning today. This chapter will examine some possible solutions. Planning must not be thought of purely as a technical exercise; if it were, planners could rely on the prescriptions offered since the war for improving the performance of town planning. There are many examples of these. As long ago as 1950 there was a Report on the qualification of planners.[2] In 1957, the Franks Report[3] criticised the volume of minor and local work on which the Ministry was engaged. In 1965, the Planning Advisory Group reported on Development Plans;[4] the Town and Country Planning Act (1968) introduced the new planning system. The 1970s saw local government reorganisation and the reform of management systems. Town planning education once again became the focus of concern, this time by a Working Group, in 1973.[5] Development control has also been the subject of enquiry.[6] The town planning profession itself established a Working Group concerned with the future of planning and this reported in 1976.[7]

My own view is somewhat different: I prefer to see planning as culturally derived, and developing within political and institutional boundaries. Planning in Britain is a twentieth–century response to the undesirable effects of industrialisation and urbanisation. Early political support was given because of the twin promise of social pacification and economic efficiency. Planning was not regarded as overtly radical; it could be accommodated within the British political system; the land market need only be marginally modified, if at all; and private interests need be no more than slightly affected. On this basis, for much of the twentieth century, planning has been an accepted feature of British and indeed western, urban society; the greater use of the State consciously to shape a future environment has suited our various social and economic arrangements. There have been fashions in regarding public sector intervention as more or less desirable, and our present period is marked by the onset of renewed doubts. Are the costs of planning justified and is the product worthwhile? With continued political shifts of this kind, planning would come to be regarded more as an optional extra to, rather than a necessary ingredient of, effective government.

The future of British town planning thus depends more on changes in its political context and its institutional setting than on changes which stem from its professional mould, or from the academic disciplines and technical skills that give it its practical content. Planning is an activity which is about choices, and it establishes goals of a kind which ultimately must win political approval. Planning may not of itself be political, but it eventually operates in a political framework. It is this fact which enables us to see the future of British planning ultimately determined by changes (marginal and incremental in all but the long term) in the context of the progress of western values and traditions. In considering the future,

The politics of town planning

I shall discuss a number of modifications to the British planning system (and its institutional arrangements), and suggest certain new approaches – not policies so much (that would be too specific for a book of this kind), but rather ways of enabling planning, a technical activity, to be an instrument of social awareness.

THE PLANNING SYSTEM

Working together

In matters of development which affect land and the environment, a feature of the British scene is that the private and public sectors are too separate, each regarding the other from ideologically fixed positions. It would be desirable to see the two sectors entering into a closer working relationship, with greater mutual trust and understanding, in planning matters. At the present time, the two sectors conspicuously fail to coordinate at points which could be most fruitful and beneficial to both. The private sector believes that in many instances the public sector interferes for wrong or insufficient reasons, and with little consequential benefit to anyone. On the other hand, the public sector is governed by a general impression that the private sector is motivated too much by individual or corporate gain, and the requirements of 'big business', that it forgets wider community interests, and may carry out development inimical to them. Under closer examination these postures are exaggerated and require modification, but the two sides are held apart to some extent because of the inherited myths surrounding them. Extreme viewpoints sour respective positions. The private sector regards the public sector as unnecessarily usurping legitimate private interests through burgeoning central bureaucracy. On the other hand the public sector regards the private sector as a rapacious exploiter, garnering profit and privilege, with no community regard. The result is that from these political attitudes about public/private postures, the development process does not operate to the full advantage of the community interest. Planning is seen as adopting a role which constrains the private sector, rather than one which works with it.

This situation must surely change if a mixed economy town planning system is to function effectively. Neither is it simply a case of the local authority providing the physical infrastructure for development, and letting the private sector 'get on with it'. There needs to be greater integration of knowledge and purpose between the public and private sectors. Urban Development Corporations, perhaps not loved by those who see them as prejudicial to the longer-term health and vitality of local government, may suggest new ways of bringing together private and public interests, powers and responsibilities. In recent years, partnership schemes (between central and local government) in respect of inner city areas pointed the way towards a greater harmony of purpose in the public sector, and in a wider respect, partnerships between local authorities and commercial interests in central area shopping developments have proved successful.

We now need to go further if that complex phenomenon, the development process, is to be fully harnessed for public and private benefit, with the community involved in the negotiated order. Structure and Local Plans have not yet achieved the coming together that is needed. Occasional developments have suggested the way forward – a housing scheme where the builder, the local community and the local authority work together, for example. The development of New Ash Green, a private enterprise village in Kent, was to have been a model; so too was Bar Hill Village near Cambridge, but both failed in their full intentions.[8]

Levels of government

It is axiomatic that local authority areas should relate not only to the functions which local government is expected to perform, but also to the type of local authority most apt to fulfil those functions. But the problem is highly complex, and objectives such as those relating to maximum democratic attainment, or to effective and efficient services, are very difficult to achieve. These were the problems which faced the Redcliffe-Maud Royal Commission on Local Government in England and which have beset local government reorganisation since 1974.

The important principle, which has great significance for town planning, is that tiers of government should enable consideration of issues, and decisions upon them, to be taken at the appropriate levels for maximum efficiency. Britain has a hierarchical system of government from Westminster (ignoring the EEC for the moment) to parish councils, with some overlap between the various levels between. Town planning is weakened because of the confusion over duplication, and in particular because of two ill-defined tiers – the region and the parish.

Town planners would argue that it is important to see forms of government at national, regional and local levels, in which major strategic issues are given greater attention at the first two, while greater opportunities are left with the local communities to guide their own development. The Local Government Act (1972) introduced an essentially two-tier system of local authorities for England and Wales: counties and districts. Since then the strategic function of counties has been considerably weakened as Structure Plans lost much of their force at a time of low economic growth and generally reduced development activity. District councils have emerged as a stronger tier, and the relative relegation of counties was further confirmed in the provisions of the Local Government Planning and Land Act (1980). The town planner attaches a particular importance to counties because of their capacity to integrate and coordinate at levels of a wider geographical scale than districts; sub regional, perhaps, if not strictly regional. Moreover, historically speaking, counties have often been of high reputation in the town planning profession, and they have assembled high grade staffs. Their disappearance, either as a deliberate act or through gradual erosion of functions, would be regrettable. Their loss could indeed only be countenanced if regrouping were effected at a truly regional level. Britain (strictly speaking, England and Wales) has no regional tier of government, but a sound case can readily be made for one. In matters relating to town planning, affecting as it does land, the environment and the allocation of resources over areas more extensive than existing units of local government, areas of socio-geographic entity need to be expressed in functional terms. These areas could be focused both on the metropolitan city regions (at the present time the metropolitan counties are too tightly conceived) and the smaller rural regions beyond, where a strategic expression in government is still required. With a proper division of functions between them, the regions and the districts could be effective tiers of local government, so permitting the intermediate counties to be extinguished.

Below the districts, community expression is poorly articulated. Much of town planning is concerned with very local matters and many of these could be dealt with locally in ways whereby small community groups might reasonably be involved. British local government has tended strongly towards large units on grounds of effectiveness. Interest in wards, parishes and neighbourhoods has been deflected accordingly, but their role needs re-emphasis. There are a sufficient number of examples on which to build; throughout this century Bournville' is an illustration of how through devices like village councils, supported by enlightened estate management, small estates or townships may take important strides towards becoming self-regulating communities.

Cities are divided into electoral areas or wards, and councillors are elected for each. Local politicians generally seem happy with the ward system, although in the absence of any proportional representation, minority parties have poor electoral results. Many wards are very large, a three member ward perhaps containing 20,000 or more inhabitants. Much smaller units representing the local neighbourhoods to which people can feel a sense of identification, called neighbourhood councils, have not received much political support, but they can be important in representing community views and in stimulating self-help and community care; however, they have no statutory status.

Parish councils, both urban and rural, appear to have more significance and potential. They have two roles: 'they are units of community feeling and community representation; and they have practical uses in economic small scale administration.'[10] They can reflect the interests and identity of a small community such as a hamlet, village, small town, suburb or housing estate. Popular support for parishes varies widely, particularly in urban areas where the creation of new parishes may be seen as a wasteful exercise. But with more delegation of powers and functions to parish councils, following the principle that responsibility for decision making should be passed down the hierarchy as far as the appropriate level permits, then effective community governance at the truly local level could become a reality. Self sufficiency and self help wherever relevant should be encouraged. Development towards, rather than away from greater community involvement in local issues should be the aim.

An interesting recent development in self help comes from Rural Voice, an alliance of national organisations representing rural communities (Council for the Protection of Rural England, Country Landowners' Association, National Association of Local Councils, National Council for Voluntary Organisations, National Farmers' Union, National Federation of Women's Institutes, National Union of Agricultural and Allied Workers and the Standing Conference of Rural Community Councils). Between them they represent over 780,000 members with branches in every village and county. Their collaboration in 1980 came in response to growing pressures on rural communities. Rural Voice obviously hopes for an understanding by government of rural problems, but the member organisations accept their own responsibility to provide leadership in the campaign to improve the quality of rural life.

The operation of the planning process

Criticisms of the present system require that it becomes more effective, more expeditious and more positive. In the achievement of these aims, two matters are crucial: the nature of development plans and the decision system.

The main weakness of both Structure Plans and Local Plans is that they rarely demonstrate fiscal realism and they fail to take cognisance of the policies of other agencies in local government and beyond. Despite the powerfully expressed views of the Planning Advisory Group, which led to the Town and Country Planning Act (1968) and the creation of the new planning system, and despite the high promise of corporate management, we still have in too many cases a land-use strategy which is imperfectly integrated with the programmes of other agencies of government.

These defects require changes. With the advent of a regional tier, county Structure Plans could be replaced by Regional Reports as currently prepared in Scotland. These bring together regional policy (in a Scottish context) expressed by all arms of government, both central and local in the region. Plans should also be reviewed each year, together with the priorities for public expenditure. These plans need not be voluminous statements; they should be limited to those essentials necessary to implement strategy; and planning developments of local significance may then be delegated to district and parish councils. Local plans similarly need to be broadly based in the sense of integrating all relevant public policy, and realistic in financial, economic and social matters.

So far as the making of decisions is concerned, criticism has focused on slowness, though overall the evidence for this is somewhat limited. Of more concern are the mechanisms for sounding out local opinion on development proposals and particularly for dealing with the power of pressure groups. A balance has to be struck between the openness of planning decisions and the speed and authority of government (of whatever tiers) in coming to final decisions. In recent years it has become apparent that too much latitude is given to groups raising objections, with the result that government has become paralysed in its actions. Objectors must be allowed to state their case, but government must equally be able to come to a decision and implement it. Pressure groups would like public funding to enable them to put their case at planning enquiries; they also seek access to data (so far confidential) on which Government may be basing its decisions. Even if these requests were met, the problem is still one of making representative democracy work. Participatory democracy does not imply the transfer of authority from properly elected representative assemblies to other non-representative bodies.

In other countries the limitations of British-style public participation have been augmented in other ways. In Australia, for example, the weight of trade union power has been brought to bear on environmental matters; in the USA advocacy planning has been adopted. Both of these have limited appeal in Britain. Adopted systems of public participation need to continue within the framework of a sharpened representative democracy, but new measures are required, particularly the early revision of the present system of inquiry procedures. In such a review it would be important to continue two trends: first, away from formal quasi-judicial inquiries to examinations of a less formal kind; second, from central levels of decision making, to regional and local levels, as appropriate.

The British Public Inquiry system has come under frequent attack in recent years, especially when major national or regional issues have been involved. The mixture of technical argument and political judgement has been hard to handle and the environmental implications have led to local unpopularity. Roads, airports, nuclear power and major construction developments of all kinds have provided the issues which the single public inquiry has not been able to resolve very well. Government has appeared to be both proponent and opponent and the inquiries have been seen as a ritual to conceal a foregone (and perhaps unpalatable) conclusion. A sense of fairness has been offended and there has been resort to civil disobedience to disrupt a public inquiry in order to prevent it being held at all. It is now necessary to admit that major projects of technological complexity and far-reaching environmental consequence need very different arrangements for public examination. To begin with, there has to be an assessment as to whether the project is needed at all (the mining of coal in the Vale of Belvoir has been challenged from this point of view, as have many other controversial projects including the Third London Airport and the Channel Tunnel). This implies consideration of national policy, and the best likely setting for this is in Select Committee, or exceptionally even in Parliament itself. Thereafter, the issues of location, siting and design can be considered in a locally held planning inquiry.

It is interesting to consider what alternatives might be adopted if the forms of public participation developed in the 1970s do not work for the 1980s. Where do we turn if participatory democracy on the lines of our present experimentation fails to convince that the costs, delays and imperfections are worthwhile? We can only speculate, but this is not a useless exercise; after all, pressure for greater public involvement came over a relatively short period, and its demise could occur just as quickly. At the moment a diffused, decentralist model of political power has wide acceptance, but there could be a return to other forms. The autocratic planning style of individuals like Peter the Great, the Popes, German Princes and other despotic monarchs is unlikely to be favoured, but equally autocratic forms of government may reappear in different collective guises. Britain may avoid these particular styles but greater political centralism may return to favour. The eighteenth–century model of enlightened patronage might return, though again under a rather different form. There may be a readiness to reject the primacy of the State in local, environmental matters in favour of other, private institutions, not presumably landed families or individuals of wealth, but corporate power, enlightened and held in Trust. The failure of the State to deliver what it promised has encouraged the participatory approach, but if this fails or disappoints, other models on these lines may prove appealing.

In the meantime, however, we should consider alternatives to public participation within our present structures for decision making. If participation proves to be too elitist because of the composition of the active pressure groups, then it would be possible to consider holding surveys or opinion polls in order to canvass local views in a truly representative way. A step in this direction came with a proposal for the legislative programme for 1982 in which the Secretary of State for the Environment had in mind referenda designed to increase the accountability of high-spending local authorities to their electorates. This follows the example of the Coventry referendum in the summer of 1981 over the question of a supplementary rate increase for that city. It would be possible to consider that all major planning applications should introduce a method of testing of this kind. Again, if participation fails, should we not consider giving more weight to the technical evidence that planning can actually provide? In other words, town planners with their technical skills could be asked to provide a better monitoring service and give guidance as to the consequences which would ensue if certain planning decisions were taken. Planners are well able to do this; at the present their knowledge is held in some suspicion, but it could happen that a reversal of attitudes takes place. Different approaches are possible, and while participation is broadly in favour today, being within the tradition of western liberalism, political structures and philosophies will alter, and speculation as to future arrangements is by no means idle.

Town planning and governance

In Britain, town planning has been slow to develop as a separate activity of local government, but since 1947 it has gathered momentum and has proved to be adaptable. The need for adaptability continues. For much of the twentieth century, town planning relied on its design bias, based on concepts of engineering and architecture. Plan making consisted of the preparation of two- or three-dimensional plans, and planning was seen in terms of land use and design. Town planning was an activity which prepared schemes, plans or layouts for future physical forms. Its method was remarkably simplistic: a threefold, linear progression from survey to analysis and plan. In the 1960s, planning began to be seen in very different terms: as part of a process of intervention in, or guidance of, a sequence of events through public policy. This led to a very different planning method, encompassing explicit formulation of objectives, evaluation of alternatives and the monitoring of results. For the town planner, process used to come second to the plan, the plan simply representing an ideal 'end state' to which process was directed. But an emphasis on long term plans changed to short term incrementalism; town planning became part of a continuous process, and this entailed a very different style of planning. The master plan was undeniably attractive because it carried authority and represented an ordered course of action, but for political reasons, reliance on this method could not be sustained. The management of a process, which recognises uncertainty as reality is much more difficult and politically demanding, yet this is the only valid stance.

The tradition of town planning has proved very useful to local government. From its early days, planning has been much more than a statutory function of government; it has been a movement with wider political significance, a profession with its own ideology and a discipline in its own right. Above all, however, it developed a synoptic nature which has permitted an integrative, coordinating role. The fact that it is orientated towards the future, together with its concern for the community and the environment, made it a useful ally of all aspects of local authority management.

Local government is part of a complex political, social and economic system. It affects the way the system operates by spending money and injecting a policy input, but does not control it (there is a multiplicity of sources for plan making). The last decade has seen strong moves towards a new role for local authorities in terms of management. Corporate planning which sought to relate activities to goals and objectives regardless of the pattern of departmental and committee responsibilities within the authority, became the new target. It recognised that problems, and the range of remedial actions that could be taken in respect of them, were complex, and that they demanded no single professional approach but a multi-skill approach. Fragmented services and policies had to be integrated and town planning was a part of the new situation.

Of immediate importance was the question of the education of those who were to be involved in management. Traditionally the people who were employed in local government were those who had been trained to do a particular job: to be an engineer, a public health inspector, a town clerk, a town planner, an educationalist or a social worker. It had to be argued that the training of all these specialist skills should have a greater awareness of relationship with other things. It also became clear that there was a need for a new type of urban administrator, who was skilled at seeing things in the round, from a corporate point of view. The service orientated professions now had to be part of teams, and they were faced with great difficulties in their educational policies. The town planner became part of the debate which expanded into a critical analysis of the role of professions in general in the late twentieth century.

Because the town planner is now engaged in urban (rural and regional) governance, he requires specialist education and training. The Amos Working Party argued for this as long ago as 1973, but little has been achieved so far.[11] The Working Party maintained that planning education had two main purposes: the development of both planning knowledge and planning capability. The various fields of planning knowledge are staggeringly wide, and selectivity is of course necessary, but nevertheless, three broad areas can be identified: knowledge about cities (and settlements of all kinds) and their communities; knowledge about organisations and processes involved in governance; and knowledge about techniques and procedures that help in governance. In 1973, it could be said that planning education focused on spatial and physical development planning, and the use of land as a resource. The Amos recommend-ation was for the development of other types of operational planning education, particularly in courses stressing social and economic problems, resources and means. In short, forms of town planning had to diversify and deepen in the interests of spatial and physical development planning. The implications of this review were that the professions engaged in planning education (primarily the Royal Town Planning Institute) should 'liberalise' their content of and approach to planning courses and permit greater specialisa-tion within a field previously seen as comprehensive and all embrac-ing. Technical expertise had to be placed in a broader social con-text. The 1970s saw significant movements in this direction, but the Amos view has fallen short of full realisation, largely because of the difficulties of coordinating the many, various control mechanisms over professional and higher education. The RTPI is by no means the only influence over the form and content of planning educa-tion; there is also the University Grants Committee, (exercising a broad view on priorities in university education), the Social Science Research Council (dictating numbers of university postgraduate en-try and evaluating individual School performances), the Council for National Academic Awards (regulating entry to polytechnics), and individual universities, polytechnics, faculties and departments (where individual preferences may be expressed about priorities). In a period of growth, changes in higher education are likely, but in a period of contraction new initiatives are very difficult to achieve. The university cuts of 1981 may result in planning education being static for some time.

This is particularly regrettable because the issues do not solely concern the content of planning education. There is also an urgent need for new forms of education beyond the undergraduate and postgraduate traditions. Mid-career, continuing education is a pressing requirement, and such is the rapidity of change within the content of knowledge, that periodic updating and mature reflection is very necessary to sensitive understanding of problems and poli-cies.

It is also important that local politicians recognise the tasks be-fore local government today. Faced as they are with the challenges of uncertainty and complexity and the need for corporate policy, they must be aware of new ideas and developments. It is equally important for the public to be educated about planning; environ-mental planning may usefully begin in schools at an early age, leading to an enhanced capacity to engage in public participation at all levels, but particularly in local situations.

Comprehensive planning

A Royal Town Planning Institute Working Party, chaired by Sylvia Law, concluded that since there are so many divisions to community governance, what is needed is a framework of inter-related planning.[12] This is a conclusion which I share. Our current failure in planning is that we have not yet devised our national machinery as an integrated whole.

Any organisation for planning reflects the organisation of the parent society. There are a number of choices society may make: for example, between a highly centralised system on the one hand, and one which leaves a good deal of freedom for people to settle their own affairs at local community level, on the other. Britain has preferred the latter course but the arrangements are neither explicit nor precise, and organisational changes in governance are needed to secure the practical benefits of it.

We have touched on some of the changes needed, but there is still one very important further gap in our planning system at the present time. Efforts directed to the conservation and management of natural resources are poorly coordinated. There is no single government department or agency charged with responsibility for natural resources, and debates about their use or conservation are often conducted in isolation. The field is a wide one: sun, wind, tide, wave, energy, air, water, fossil fuels and minerals. We are so far not familiar with energy use planning and planning at the interface between land and energy has been very crude indeed. We are unsure of the relationship between urban form (particularly density) and energy requirements, and we are only beginning to appreciate the environmental impacts of various energy developments. Our planning system has got bogged down in inquiries in respect of proposals for major energy developments; this has highlighted not only our relative ignorance about the physical, economic, social and environmental impacts, but also the fact that our national and local planning systems are discordant. We need a national policy with regard to energy and natural resources. But the impact of development is to be felt locally, and the local planning system has been under impossible strain in dealing with both national and local interests. The ways in which our decisions are being taken seem to be haphazard and are causing public dissatisfaction. An integrated framework for national strategy and local planning guidelines is required, as MacLeary has recently argued.[13]

OBJECTIVES FOR PLANNING

Thus modifications are needed to certain features of our planning system and the institutional framework through which they operate. We have suggested that new approaches might include greater coordination of purpose between the public, private and voluntary sectors, attention to levels of government where planning is currently weak, technical adjustments in plan preparation, a recognition that town planning is one of the tools of urban governance, and a plea for some measure of comprehensive planning, particularly in matters concerning natural resources and energy.

These suggestions relate to the current planning system, but they do not spell out the actual objectives of town planning: what sort of society, what sort of environment are we to plan for? What are the aims of town planning today? What are the end products which the system is designed to achieve? In previous decades answers to these questions could be given fairly readily. Unwin, for example, could offer his new forms of residential architecture for future generations; Abercrombie could present his grand spatial models for cities; planners of the mid 1960s articulated their technological superiority in terms of growth axes and impressive sweeps of land distribution patterns. Moreover, throughout the century planners could point to the relationship between the nature and quality of the physical environment on the one hand and the community which experienced it on the other: qualitative improvements in the environment surely contributed to human happiness.

Few would feel comfortable today in expressing the objectives of town planning in these terms, although aims to secure the 'right use of land' through the creative control over myriad acts of private development in the public interest, and to seek the visual enhancement of the physical environment, still rest at the heart of the land planner's task. The difficulty is in offering dramatic, imaginative and tangible objectives about the future city and the countryside. In the past it was easier, but purely physical goals for the next generation cannot be on today's agenda. The unrealistic claims in the past have only led to disappointment and disillusionment. For the rest of the century we must resist the idea that town planning can be identified from within its own philosophy, as offering cut and dried solutions for our towns, cities, regions and countryside in terms of layout, design, structure or distribution. Town planning will still be part of a system of governance which will attempt some measure of control over the built environment and its development, but it will not hold any single, magical key of reconstruction.

However, there must be a general aim at some tangible and attainable target, otherwise town planning degenerates into 'planning for planning's sake' and there is substance in the charge that planning has become process without purpose. Incrementalism without wider objectives does not gain support for long. In fact land-use planning in recent years has lost a sense of direction, buffetted by demographic and economic change, political vaccillation and the withdrawal of popular approval. It is timely for professionals to demonstrate rather more convincingly what they want to achieve and why, and to ensure that the process of getting it meets with community support.

At the outset it has to be acknowledged that whereas in the past town planning was 'place based', it now has to be 'people based'. There are, of course, dangers in holding this view to the exclusion of any spatial acknowledgement. It is true that in earlier decades this century town planning had a physical, spatial, environmental and visual base; social and other policies were somehow expected to fit these other criteria. But we must not now fall into the trap of discounting the spatial consequences of our contemporary range of housing and other social welfare programmes. The fact is that social policies need to recognise spatial implications just as much as spatial policies need to recognise social implications. Nonetheless, planning professionals do have to acknowledge important changes in their subject field and the nature of their work. Problems have changed; parameters have changed. The future of town planning is not bound to a single profession with an unchanging, historically determined remit. An interdisciplinary prospect is surely in store. An overriding concern for spatial distributions and the 'rightness' of particular forms of environmental design may have been very appropriate in the past (although critics may now say that these concerns only served to conceal concerns for other factors, essentially social and political, but non-spatial in their incidence). But for the future, town planning has to relate as much to people as to places. In other words, town planning will have much common ground with what might now be described as urban social policy, itself having moved out of the tighter frame of social administration.

Disciplinary and professional labels are being redefined. At a time when public policy, environmental planning and forms of social and economic policy are so much in flux, it may be suggested with some confidence that the future evolution of town planning will lead to a set of rather different jobs for its practitioners. An indication of the developing approach might be seen in President Carter's policy statement following the Report of the President's Urban and Regional Policy Group; the US Government issued its first National Urban Policy in March 1978. The policies make highly relevant reading for British urban planners: improvements in local planning and administration; fiscal assistance to distressed areas; State involvement in urban aid; greater participation of community groups; upgrading the physical and cultural infrastructure of the urban environment; greater incentives for private investment in cities; aid to the disadvantaged; help to the long-term unemployed; and better health and social service provision. This in large measure could be a British agenda too, and it is important to note the almost indissoluble links between spatial and non-spatial policies. Many sectoral policies will be spatially significant: for example, it can be argued that subsidies (via tax relief) to new, middle-income housing have fuelled a substantial demand for extensive suburban spread. Conversely, spatial and environmental policies will have social significance. As an illustration, the town planner has to ask (for example, with respect to the inner city) why it is important: as a place to design and manage as an improved environment, or for people who happen to live there? The urban policy maker has to acknowledge that his package of housing, social and economic policies will not be spatially neutral in the dynamic metropolitan structure of which the inner city is part.

The planner's professional remit is evolving. For the foreseeable future it will be necessary for his past preoccupation with space and the physical attributes of the built environment to be at least shared with a wider set of related, non-spatial concerns. Not that the implication is that the townplanner necessarily becomes the jack of all trades or that he becomes the philosopher-king; specialisms will remain, but a balance will be struck. The planner's basic interest in land policy and environmental management will continue, but it will be impossible for a professional role to remain confined to this area. A wider, interpenetrative fusion to a concern with social welfare will be required. In this context, planners might begin to articulate a new sense of purpose with a simple but profound observation: borrowing from a prayer of St Francis of Assisi, we may say that the planner's task is 'not so much to be understood but to understand'. This is to imply that the planner's job is to comprehend, interpret and then help to mould what is going on around him, rather than to determine from within his own convictions a societal and environmental future, and then seek to impose it on his and future generations. As a social scientist he assesses his contemporary world; as a socio-political analyst he assists in the process of problem identification; as a builder he helps to shape a physical world for community benefit.

Previous generations have done just this. A mirror was held up to the late Victorian city and its housing, health, social and environmental problems were made the targets for reform. The new town planning offered its solutions in land management and housing improvements. In the mid 1940s the old and the obsolete in the environment and the relics of the nineteenth–century conurbations were finally to be swept away in programmes of decentralisation, dispersal and urban renewal. But the targets of each generation become outmoded: at the beginning of the 1980s no new dramatic target has emerged.

We still pretend that our planning system is shaping the distributional map of urban Britain, controlling urban growth and guiding regional destinies. But this is a pretence: it is now fairly clear that in Britain and the market economy countries of the West public sector, land policies have remarkably little effect at macro scale on the shaping of metropolitan form and regional distributional patterns. This is not to say that at relatively local scale modest adjustments cannot and do not occur, rather that we cannot harness land planning to do much, on its own, towards shaping our future city. Hall and Hay have recently given a statistical analysis of the European urban system.[14] Atlantic Europe (Great Britain and Ireland) is undergoing 'a remarkable degree of population decentralisation: relatively in the 1950s, in the sense that rings were gaining on cores; absolutely in the 1960s and 1970s, in the sense that core populations were actually falling, and falling at a rapidly increasing rate.' In the 1970s, widely diffused growth was taking place around London extending far into East Anglia and to Devon and Cornwall. Population losses in the big cities was noticeable in London, Birmingham, Manchester, Liverpool and Glasgow. In the northern half of the country stagnation or decline was the norm. Britain is, in fact, of all European regions, nearest to the American model of the regional, dispersed city. The inter-related forces of change which are creating this new pattern are extraordinarily complex and it is unlikely that any switching of financial resources by the public sector would make any significant result. All countries in Western Europe have operated land-use policies since the war – regional development, urban growth strategies, moves to establish or relocate industry – but Hall and Hay consider that there is 'no basis for a belief that regional policies or patterns of transfer of fiscal resources between local authorities had influenced patterns of change.'

We do not look to town planning therefore for dramatic new spatial models for urban life. By itself, it seems to have very limited influence over patterns of distribution at macro scale. When the tide of other forces are running in its favour then town planning can be very successful, but it is unlikely to be so without them.

Another line of argument is that the ideal city could be reached through a particular political system, different from our own. However, from our mixed, public-private sector perspective, other alternatives do not look terribly attractive. For example, there seems little to recommend in the drabness of the socialist city. Bater[15] has written of the unfavourable pattern of daily life (to Western eyes, that is), the social costs of the housing shortage and the other environmental costs of aspects of Soviet town planning. Other sources give a similar impression.[16]

What sort of role is most appropriate for town planning at this point of the century? Grand strategic sweeps may appear on our agenda again – but not now. Planning at a time of economic retrenchment imposes restraints and obliges the planning system to focus on the incrementalism of urban and community management: this is the new realism of planning. This is forced upon us by our analysis of the planning system: the necessary recognition of pluralism, the politics of organisational structures, and the conclusion that comprehensive, long-term spatial planning rarely achieves very much. The physical objectives of town planning today are therefore relatively small scale and local in impact: they are very much concerned with the management of the development process, not just as a passive regulator but as a positive agent of change in (and by) the public sector. This seems to be the late twentieth–century role of town planning.

But what confidence can we have that town planning will carry community support? Is it not precisely in its development role that planning has incurred so much community hostility? An important rider must therefore be introduced: town planning's performance in the development process must be guided by new attitudes if it is to avoid the mistakes of the last twenty years when forms of exploitative, 'clean-sweep' planning seemed to deny so much that the community chose to value. In her study of post-war urban planning Alison Ravetz argues that a change of attitudes is necessary if we are to behave differently towards the environment: instead of flouting and wasting it, we must seek out and enhance its richness and variety.[17] The planner himself with his humanistic outlook can be instrumental in the rediscovery of the importance of the environment.

Ravetz considers the prescription for the future to lie in principles which emphasise respect for life and respect for culture. She stresses the importance of inner significance before outer form. These principles have implications for forms of environmental planning, and we may suggest them as the broad targets for town planning in its contemporary role. Respect for life and culture means a bias towards conservation and against wholesale and unnecessary destruction. Concern for personal responsibility means following social and technological systems where human identity can be preserved: in short, a presumption against the massive and the depersonalised. An awareness of the limits to our knowledge leads us into humility when we are exercising power over others (either technological or political).

The plea therefore is for town planning, a technical job framed by social awareness, to be guided by ideas and ideals which will positively contribute to the sum of human happiness; in this task respect for the individual should have primacy. Thirty years of urban reshaping on a vast scale have come to an end. The next ten years at least are going to be very different. Town planning has a relatively modest but very important task before it: it is not called upon to dream dreams for the future or to prepare great plans. But its more limited role is surely more attainable: it must be the ever-close scrutinisor of the changing world and the built environment, the agent or animator of desirable development, and the respector both of people and the natural world.

This is an enabling philosophy. It suggests targets which are centred around people, and it entails technical activity which is harnessed to social purpose. Moreover, it is the common denominator of many of the suggestions made earlier: improved housing provision and careful attention to an ageing stock; employment generation and new forms of economic planning at local scale; the wise management of transportation systems to create spatially functional cities; planning for leisure; the stewardship of natural resources; the furthering of participatory democracy and the decentralisation of government to the lowest appropriate levels; and the pursuit of all that enhances the quality of the environment.

These matters may form an unsurprising agenda, but the issues with which they are concerned constitute the politics of town planning. If these issues can be tackled with imagination, humility and respect for human values, then the benefit to society will be very great.

REFERENCES

Chapter 1 Town planning and the political dimension

1. CHERRY, GORDON E. (1979) 'The town planning movement and the late Victorian city', *Transactions, The Institute of British Geographers*, Vol. 4, No. 2.
2. HALL, PETER, *et al.* (1973) *The Containment of Urban England*, Vol. 2, George Allen and Unwin, London.
3. FRASER, D. (1973) *The Evolution of the British Welfare State*, Macmillan, London.
4. HEAP, SIR DESMOND (1975) *The Land and the Development*, Stevens, London.
5. HENNOCK, E. P. (1973) *Fit and Proper Persons, ideal and reality in nineteenth-century government*, Edward Arnold, London.
6. CHAMBERLAIN, JOSEPH 'State socialism and the moderate liberals', 28 April 1885, in C.W. Boyd, (ed.) *Speeches I*. Quoted in Hennock, *op. cit.*
7. CHERRY, GORDON E. (1980) 'The place of Neville Chamberlain in British town planning', in Gordon E. Cherry (ed.) *Shaping an Urban World: Planning in the Twentieth Century*, Mansell, London.
8. FRASER, DEREK (1979) *Power and Authority in the Victorian City*, Basil Blackwell, Oxford.
9. WOODS, ROBERT (1978) 'Mortality and sanitary conditions in the "Best governed city in the world" – Birmingham, 1870–1910', *Journal of Historical Geography*, Vol. 4, No. 1.
10. CHERRY, GORDON E. (1974) *The Evolution of British Town Planning*, Leonard Hill, Heath and Reach.
11. BARNETT, CANON and MRS S. A. (1909) *Towards Social Reform*, T. Fisher Unwin, London.
12. BARNETT CANON (1979) *The Ideal City*, Helen M. Meller (ed.), Leicester University Press, Leicester.

13. FOSTER, JOHN (1979) 'How imperial London preserved its slums', *International Journal of Urban and Regional Research*, Vol. 3, No. 1.

Chapter 2   Developments in town planning – pre-1939

1. CHERRY, GORDON E. (1975) *Factors in the Origins of Town Planning in Britain: the example of Birmingham 1905–14*, Working Paper 36, Centre for Urban and Regional Studies, University of Birmingham.
2. BROWN, KENNETH D. (1977) *John Burns*, Royal Historical Society, London.
3. KENT, WILLIAM (1950) *John Burns: Labour's Lost Leader*, Williams and Norgate, London.
4. CHERRY, GORDON E. (1974) *The Evolution of British Town Planning*, Leonard Hill, Heath and Reach.
5. This section is based on MINETT, JOHN (1974) 'The Housing, Town Planning etc. Act, 1909', *The Planner*, Vol. 60, May.
6. CHERRY, GORDON E. *op. cit.* (1).
7. This section is based on CHERRY, GORDON E. (1974) 'The Housing Town Planning etc. Act, 1919', *The Planner*, Vol. 60, May.
8. This section is based on WARD, STEPHEN (1974) 'The Town and Country Planning Act, 1932', *The Planner*, Vol. 60, May.
9. KENNETT, WAYLAND (1972) *Preservation*, Temple Smith, London.
10. WARD, STEPHEN *op. cit.* (8).
11. CHERRY, GORDON E. (1980) 'The place of Neville Chamberlain in British town planning', Gordon E. Cherry (ed.) *Shaping an Urban World: Planning in the Twentieth Century*, Mansell, London.
12. Greater London Regional Planning Committee, *minutes* of first meeting, 2 Nov. 1927.
13. DONOGHUE, BERNARD and JONES, G. W. (1973) *Herbert Morrison, Portrait of a Politician*, Weidenfeld and Nicolson, London.
14. SHEAIL, J. (1979) 'The Restriction of Ribbon Development Act: the character and perception of land use control in inter war Britain', *Regional Studies*, Vol. 13, No. 6.
15. CHERRY, GORDON E. (1975) *Environmental Planning, Vol. II, National Parks and Recreation in the Countryside*, HMSO, London.

Chapter 3   Developments in town planning – war-time and post-war

1. ROWNTREE, B. SEEBOHM (1941) *Poverty and Progress: a second social survey of York*, Longmans, Green, London.
2. WOMEN'S GROUP ON PUBLIC WELFARE (1943) *Our Towns: a close up*, Oxford University Press, London.
3. CULLINGWORTH, J. B. (1975) *Environmental Planning, Vol. I, Reconstruction and Land Use Planning, 1939–1947*, HMSO, London.
4. STUART, CHARLES (1975) *The Reith Diaries*, Collins, London.
5. REITH, J. C. W. (1949) *Into the Wind*, Hodder and Stoughton, London.
6. CULLINGWORTH, J. B., *op. cit.* (3).
7. *Ibid.*
8. FOOT, MICHAEL (1962) *Aneurin Bevan*, Vol. I, 1897–1945, Macgibbon and Kee, London.
9. FOOT, MICHAEL, *op. cit.*
10. JOHNSTON, THOMAS (1952) *Memories*, Collins, London.
11. SIMON, E. D. (1945) *Rebuilding Britain – a Twenty Year Plan*, Victor Gollancz, London.
12. DALTON, H. (1957) *The Fateful Years: Memoirs 1931–1945*, Muller, London.
13. CULLINGWORTH, J. B. (1979) *Environmental Planning, Vol. III, New Towns Policy*, HMSO, London.
14. CULLINGWORTH, J. B., *op. cit.* (13).
15. CHERRY, GORDON E. (1975) *Environmental Planning, Vol. II, National Parks and Recreation in the Countryside*, HMSO, London.
16. YOUNG, MICHAEL and WILLMOTT, PETER (1957) *Family and Kinship in East London*, Routledge & Kegan Paul, London.
17. CROSSMAN, RICHARD (1975) *The Diaries of a Cabinet Minister* (3 vols), Vol. I, Hamish Hamilton and Jonathan Cape, London.
18. For example, CULLINGWORTH, J. B. (1964–76), *Town and Country Planning in Britain*, George Allen & Unwin, London.
19. LEUNG HOK LIN (1979) *Redistribution of Land Values*, Occasional Paper No. 11, Department of Land Economy, University of Cambridge.
20. CULLINGWORTH, J. B. (1979) *op. cit.* (13).
21. TAYLOR, NICHOLAS (1973) *The Village in the City*, Maurice Temple Smith, London.

22. YOUNG, K. (1972) 'Political party organisation' in Gerald Rhodes (ed.) *The New Government of London*, Weidenfeld and Nicholson, London.
23. DAVIES, JON GOWER (1972) *The Evangelistic Bureaucrat*, Tavistock, London.
24. DENNIS, N. (1970) *People and Planning*, Faber, London.
25. SMITH, DAN (1970) *An Autobiography*, Oriel Press, Newcastle upon Tyne, 1970.
26. HUMBLE, STEPHEN (1978) 'Sir Michael Higgs: the old Worcestershire and the new Hereford and Worcester'; SUTCLIFFE, ANTHONY, 'Harry Watton and Stan Yapp, contrasting styles of leadership in Labour controlled Birmingham', in G. W. Jones and Alan Norton (eds), *Political Leadership in Local Authorities*, Institute of Local Government Studies, University of Birmingham.
27. CROSLAND, ANTHONY, 'Protecting the environment', in *Socialism Now*, Jonathan Cape, London, 1974.
28. EDWARDS, JOHN and BATLEY, RICHARD (1978) *The Politics of Positive Discrimination*, Tavistock, London.

Chapter 4   Political approaches towards town planning

1. WHITE, PAUL M. (1980) *Soviet Urban and Regional Planning*, Mansell, London.
2. BRUCE, MAURICE (1973) (ed.) *The Rise of the Welfare State, English Social Policy, 1601–1971*, Weidenfeld and Nicolson, London.
3. WILSON, JOHN (1973) *C. B. A Life of Sir Henry Campbell-Bannerman*, Constable, London.
4. FOOT, MICHAEL (1962) *Aneurin Bevan*, Vol. I, Macgibbon and Kee, London.
5. SIMON, E. D. (1929) *How to Abolish the Slums*, Longmans, Green, London.
6. SIMON, E. D. (1933) *The Anti-Slum Campaign*, Longmans, Green, London.
7. HARDY, DENNIS (1979) *Alternative Communities in Nineteenth Century England*, Longman, Harlow.
8. RYE, JANE (1972) *Futurism*, Studio Vista, London.
9. LANSBURY, GEORGE (1934) *My England*, Selwyn and Blount, London.
10. MIDDLEMASS, ROBERT KEITH (1965) *The Clydesiders*, Hutchinson, London.

11. JOHNSTON, THOMAS (1952) *Memories*, Collins, London.

12. POTTINGER, GEORGE (1979) *The Secretaries of State for Scotland 1926–76*, Scottish Academic Press, Edinburgh.

13. SILKIN, LEWIS (1943) *The Nation's Land*, Fabian Publications, Research Series 70, London.

14. SILKIN, LEWIS (1946) 'Our plan for land and houses', in *Forward From Victory!*, Victor Gollancz, London.

15. CHERRY, GORDON E. (1980) 'The place of Neville Chamberlain in British town planning', in Gordon E. Cherry (ed.) *Shaping an Urban World: Planning in the Twentieth Century*, Mansell, London.

16. SIMON, E. D. and INMAN, J. (1935) *The Rebuilding of Manchester*, Longmans, Green, London.

17. BEALEY, FRANK (1970) (ed.) *The Social and Political Thought of the British Labour Party*, Weidenfeld and Nicolson, London.

18. MIDDLEMAS, KEITH (1969) (ed.) *Whitehall Diary*, Vol. II, Oxford University Press, London.

19. MACMILLAN, HAROLD (1938) *The Middle Way*, Macmillan, London.

20. SIMON, SIR ERNEST (1937) *Report* of the Town and Country Planning Summer School, Town Planning Institute, London.

21. WALKER, PETER (1977) *The Ascent of Britain*, Sidgwick and Jackson, London.

22. GRIMOND, JOSEPH (1963) *The Liberal Challenge*, Hollis and Carter, London.

23. GRIMOND, JOSEPH (1978) *The Common Welfare*, Maurice Temple Smith, London.

24. CROSLAND, C. A. R. (1956) *The Future of Socialism*, Jonathan Cape, London.

25. FOWLER, GERRY (1967) 'Planning for the population of the future', in Ben Whitaker (ed.) *A Radical Future*, Jonathan Cape, London.

26. SHORE, PETER (1958) 'In the room at the top', in Norman Mackenzie (ed.) *Conviction*, MacGibbon and Kee, London.

27. SHORE, PETER (1980) *Urban Decay: its Symptoms and Remedies*, The Thomas Cubitt Trust, London.

28. HATTERSLEY, ROY (1976) *Goodbye to Yorkshire*, Victor Gollancz, London; Penguin (1978).

29. SECRETARY OF STATE FOR THE ENVIRONMENT (1979), Speech, University of York, Town and Country Planning Summer School, *mimeo*, 13 Sept.

30. JOSEPH, SIR KEITH (1974) 'The continuing heritage', RIBA/ Civic Trust Conference.
31. RICHARDSON, KENNETH (1972) *Twentieth Century Coventry*, Macmillan, London.
32. HODGKINSON, GEORGE (1970) *Sent to Coventry*, Robert Maxwell.
33. SMITH, DAN (1970) *An Autobiography*, Oriel Press, Newcastle upon Tyne.
34. WILKES, LYALL and DODDS, GORDON (1964) *Tyneside Classical*, John Murray, London.

Chapter 5   Planning and politics in practice

1. WILSON, HAROLD (1976) *The Governance of Britain*, Weidenfeld and Nicolson, London.
2. BLOWERS, ANDREW (1980) *The Limits of Power*, Pergamon Press, Oxford.
3. HALL, PETER (1980) *Great Planning Disasters*, Weidenfeld and Nicolson, London.
4. *Final Report of the New Towns Committee*, (1946) Cmd 6876, HMSO.
5. MULLAN, BOB (1980) *Stevenage Ltd. Aspects of the planning and politics of Stevenage New Town, 1945–78*, Routledge & Kegan Paul, London.
6. GOURSOLAS, JEAN–MARC (1980) 'New Towns in the Paris metropolitan area', *International Journal of Urban and Regional Research*, Vol. 4, No. 3.
7. NINER, PAT and WATSON, CHRISTOPHER J. (1978) 'Housing in British cities', in D. T. Herbert and R. J. Johnston (eds) *Geography and the Urban Environment: progress in research applications*, Vol. I, John Wiley, Chichester.
8. CULLINGWORTH, J. B. (1981) *Environmental Planning, Vol. IV, Land Values, Compensation and Betterment*, HMSO, London.
9. DENMAN, DONALD (1980) *Land in a Free Society*, Centre for Policy Studies, London.
10. SANDBACH, FRANCIS (1980) *Environment, Ideology and Policy*, Basil Blackwell, Oxford.
11. JOHNSON, TERENCE J. (1972) *Professions and Power*, Macmillan, London.
12. MCAUSLAN, PATRICK (1980) *The Ideologies of Planning Law*, Pergamon Press, Oxford.

13. REGAN, D. E. (1978) 'The pathology of British land use planning', *Local Government Studies*, Vol. 4, No. 2.
14. SANDBACH, FRANCIS (1980 a) *op. cit.*
15. SANDBACH, FRANCIS (1980) 'The early campaign for a National Park in the Lake District', in Roger Kain (ed.) *Planning for Conservation*, Mansell.
16. SHOARD, MARION (1980) *The Theft of the Countryside*, Temple Smith, London.
17. HALL, PETER (1980) *op. cit.*
18. GREGORY, ROY (1971) *The Price of Amenity*, Macmillan, London.
19. NEWMAN, ROLAND (1980) *The Road and Christchurch Meadow*, Oxford Polytechnic.
20. KIMBER, RICHARD and RICHARDSON, J. J. (eds.) (1974) *Campaigning for the Environment*, Routledge & Kegan Paul, London.
21. MOSS, GRAHAM (1981) *Britain's Wasting Acres: land use in a changing environment*, The Architectural Press, London.
22. GYFORD, JOHN (1976) *Local Politics in Britain*, Croom Helm, London.
23. DAVIES, J. G. (1972) *The Evangelistic Bureaucrat*, Tavistock, London.
24. DENNIS, N. (1972) *Public Participation and Planners' Blight*, Faber, London.
25. RAVETZ, ALISON (1980) *Remaking Cities*, Croom Helm, London.
26. CHRISTENSEN, TERRY (1979) *Neighbourhood Survival: the struggle for Covent Garden's future*, Prism Press, London.
27. GOLDSMITH, MICHAEL (1980) *Politics, Planning and the City*, Hutchinson, London.
28. CHERRY, GORDON E. (1975) *Environmental Planning, Vol. II, National Parks and Recreation in the Countryside*, HMSO.
29. CHERRY, GORDON E. (1980) 'Prospects for regional planning – a review of metropolitan strategies for the West Midlands', *Local Government Studies*, Vol. 6, No. 3, May/June.
30. SHEAIL, JOHN (1980) 'Changing perceptions of land–use controls in inter–war Britain', in Roger Kain (ed.) *Planning for Conservation*, Mansell, London.
31. MCKAY, DAVID H. and COX, ANDREW W. (1979) *The Politics of Urban Change*, Croom Helm, London.
32. CROSBY, ALAN (1980) *The Experience of Gradual Renewal in the Jericho District of Oxford*, Research Paper 25, School of

Geography, University of Oxford.
33. LOWERSON, JOHN (1980) 'Battles for the countryside', in Frank Gloversmith, (ed.) *Class, Culture and Social Change*, Harvester Press, Brighton.
34. SHOARD, MARION (1980) *op. cit.*
35. MURIE, ALAN; NINER, PAT; and WATSON, CHRISTOPHER (1976) *Housing Policy and the Housing System*, George Allen & Unwin, London.
36. LANSLEY, STEWART (1979) *Housing and Public Policy*, Croom Helm, London.
37. DUNN, MICHAEL; RAWSON, MARILYN; and ROGERS, ALAN (1981) *Rural Housing: Competition and Choice*, George Allen & Unwin, London.
38. SHELTER (1980) *And I'll Blow Your House Down*, London.
39. HOLTERMANN, S. (1975) 'Areas of urban deprivation in Great Britain: an analysis of 1971 census data', *Social Studies*, Vol. 6, HMSO, London.
40. LAWLESS, PAUL (1979) *Urban Deprivation and Government Initiative*, Faber, London.
41. KIRBY, ANDREW (1978) *The Inner City: causes and effects*, Retailing and Planning Associates, Corbridge, Northumberland.
42. LAWLESS, PAUL (1979) *op. cit.*
43. FRIEND, ANDREW and METCALF, ANDY (1981) *Slump City: the politics of mass unemployment*, Pluto Press, London.
44. MAWSON, JOHN (1981) 'Changing directions in regional policy and the implications for Local Government', *Local Government Studies*, Annual Review.
45. TYME, JOHN (1978) *Motorways versus Democracy: public inquiries into road proposals and their political significance*, Macmillan, London.
46. THOMSON, J. MICHAEL (1977) *Great Cities and their Traffic*, Victor Gollancz, London.
47. O'RIORDAN, TIMOTHY (1981) 'Environmentalism and education', *Journal of Geography in Higher Education*, Vol. 5, No. 1.
48. SMITH, PETER J. (1975) *The Politics of Physical Resources*, Penguin, Harmondsworth.
49. NEWBY, HOWARD (1979) *Green and Pleasant Land? Social change in rural England*, Hutchinson, London.
50. DENMAN, DONALD (1980) *op. cit.*

Chapter 6   Today's political questions

1. *Planning and the Future* (1976) The Royal Town Planning Institute, London.
2. *Party Politics in Local Government: officers and members* (1980) Royal Institute of Public Administration and Policy Studies Institute.
3. BUDD, ALAN (1978) *The Politics of Economic Planning*, Fontana, London.
4. CASTELLS, MANUEL (1977) 'Towards a political urban sociology', in Michael Harloe (ed.) *Captive Cities: studies in the political economy of cities and regions*, John Wiley, Chichester.
5. SIMMIE, JAMES (1981) *Power, Property and Corporatism: the political sociology of planning*, Macmillan, London.
6. COCKBURN, CYNTHIA (1977) *The Local State: management of cities and people*, Pluto Press, London.
7. PAHL, R. E. (1975) 'Urban managerialism reconsidered', in *Whose City?* Penguin, London. See also PAHL, R. E. (1977) 'Managers, technical experts and the State: forms of mediation, manipulation and dominance in urban and regional development', in Michael Harloe (ed.) *Captive Cities*.
8. MCKAY, DAVID H. and COX, ANDREW W. (1979) *The Politics of Urban Change*, Croom Helm, London.
9. KIRK, GWYNETH (1980) *Urban Planning in a Capitalist Society*, Croom Helm, London.
10. MINGIONE, ENZO (1981) *Social Conflict and the City*, Basil Blackwell, Oxford.
11. CHERRY, GORDON E. (1978) 'Prospects for the profession', *The Planner*, Vol. 64, No. 6.
12. *People and Planning* (1969) Committee on Public Participation in Planning (the Skeffington Report), HMSO, London.
13. STEWART, J. D. (1958) *British Pressure Groups: their role in relation to the House of Commons*, Clarendon Press, Oxford.
14. SEWELL, W. R. D. and COPPOCK, J. T. (eds) (1977) *Public Participation in Planning*, John Wiley, Chichester.
15. TYME, JOHN (1978) *Motorways versus Democracy*, Macmillan, London.
16. TWINN, IAN D. (1978) *Public Involvement or Public Protest: a case study of the M3 at Winchester 1971–74*, Polytechnic of the South Bank.
17 HAIN, PETER (1976) *Community Politics*, John Calder, London.

18. ELKIN, STEPHEN L. (1974) *Politics and Land Use Planning: the London experience*, Cambridge University Press.

19. *Royal Commission on Local Government in England* (Redcliffe-Maud Report) (1969) Vol. 1, Cmnd 4040, London.

20. *Op. cit.* Vol. 2, Memorandum of Dissent, D. Senior.

21. *The Reorganisation of Central Government* (1970) Cmnd 4506, HMSO, London.

22. *Local Government in England* (1971) Cmnd 4584, HMSO, London.

23. STEWART, J. D. (1980) 'The governance of the conurbations', in Gordon C. Cameron (ed.) *The Future of the British Conurbations*, Longman, Harlow.

24. STEWART, J. D. (1974) *The Responsive Local Authority*, Charles Knight, London.

25. *Management of Local Government*, Maud Report (1967) HMSO, London.

26. *The New Local Authorities: Management and Structure* (1972) Bains Report, HMSO, London.

27. BLOWERS, ANDREW, *op. cit.*

Chapter 7   Facing the future

1. DONNISON, DAVID with SOTO, PAUL (1980) *The Good City: a study of urban development and policy in Britain*, Heinemann, London.

2. *Report of the Committee on the Qualifications of Planners* (1950) Cmd 8059, HMSO, London.

3. *Report of the Committee on Administrative Tribunals and Enquiries*, (1957) Cmnd 218, HMSO, London.

4. *The Future of Development Plans* (1965) Report by the Planning Advisory Group, HMSO, London.

5. *Education for Planning* (1973) Report of a working group at the Centre for Environmental Studies, Progress in Planning, Vol. 1, Part 1, Pergamon Press Oxford.

6. *Review of the Development Control System* (1974, 1975) Dobry Reports, HMSO.

7. *Planning and the Future* (1976) Discussion paper of a working group established by the Royal Town Planning Institute (RTPI) London.

8. DARLEY, GILLIAN (1975) *Villages of Vision*, The Architectural Press, London.

9. *The Bournville Village Trust 1900–1955* (1955) BVT, Birmingham.

10. Circular 121/77, Department of the Environment, 12 Dec. 1977.

11. *Education for Planners, op. cit.*

12. *Planning and the Future, op. cit.*

13. MACLEARY, ALISTAIR (1980) 'Energy and land use in the United Kingdom', in *Planning and Energy*, International Society of City and Regional Planners, Zurich, 1980 (Strasbourg Congress, 1979).

14. HALL, PETER and HAY, DENNIS (1980) *Growth Centres in the European Urban System*, Heinemann, London.

15. BATER, JAMES H. (1980) *The Soviet City*, Edward Arnold, London.

16. FRENCH, R. A. and HAMILTON, F. E. IAN (1979) *The Socialist City*, John Wiley, Chichester.

17. RAVETZ, ALISON (1980) *Remaking Cities*, Croom Helm, London.

SELECT BIBLIOGRAPHY

TWENTIETH-CENTURY PLANNING

CHERRY, GORDON E., *The Evolution of British Town Planning*, Leonard Hill, Heath and Reach, 1974.

CULLINGWORTH, J. B., *Town and Country Planning in Britain*, George Allen and Unwin, London, 1964–76.

HALL, PETER, *et al*, *The Containment of Urban England*, Vol. 2, George Allen and Unwin, London, 1973.

Peacetime Histories

CULLINGWORTH, J. B., *Environmental Planning, Vol. I, Reconstruction and Land Use Planning, 1939–1947*, HMSO, London, 1975.

CHERRY, GORDON E., *Environmental Planning, Vol. II, National Parks and Recreation in the Countryside*, HMSO, London, 1975.

CULLINGWORTH, J. B., *Environmental Planning, Vol. III, New Towns Policy*, HMSO, London, 1979.

CULLINGWORTH, J. B., *Environmental Planning, Vol. IV, Land Values, Compensation and Betterment*, HMSO, London, 1981.

POST-WAR PLANNING CRITIQUES

BLOWERS, ANDREW, *The Limits of Power*, Pergamon Press, Oxford, 1980.

EDWARDS, JOHN, and BATLEY, RICHARD, *The Politics of Positive Discrimination*, Tavistock, London, 1978.

GREGORY, ROY, *The Price of Amenity*, Macmillan, London, 1971.

HALL, PETER, *Great Planning Disasters*, Weidenfeld and Nicolson, London, 1980.

MCKAY, DAVID H. and COX, ANDREW W., *The Politics of Urban Change*, Croom Helm, London, 1979.

RAVETZ, ALISON, *Remaking Cities*, Croom Helm, London, 1980.

SHOARD, MARION, *The Theft of the Countryside*, Temple Smith, London, 1980.

YOUNG, MICHAEL and WILLMOTT, PETER, *Family and Kinship in East London*, Routledge and Kegan Paul, London, 1957.

URBAN POLITICS

CASTELLS, MANUEL, 'Towards a Political Urban Sociology', in Harloe, Michael (ed) *Captive Cities: studies in the political economy of cities and regions*, John Wiley, Chichester, 1977.

COCKBURN, CYNTHIA, *The Local State: management of cities and people*, Pluto Press, London, 1977.

GOLDSMITH, MICHAEL, *Politics, Planning and the City*, Hutchinson, London, 1980.

PAHL, R. E., 'Urban Managerialism Reconsidered', in *Whose City?* Penguin, London, 1975.

PLANNING AND THE PUBLIC

DAVIES, JON GOWER, *The Evangelistic Bureaucrat*, Tavistock, London, 1972.

DENNIS, N., *Public Participation and Planners' Blight*, Faber, London, 1972.

SEWELL, W. R. D. and COPPOCK, J. T. (eds), *Public Participation in Planning*, John Wiley, Chichester, 1977.

People and Planning, Committee on Public Participation in Planning (the Skeffington Report), HMSO, London, 1969.

TYME, JOHN, *Motorways versus Democracy: public inquiries into road proposals and their political significance*, Macmillan, London, 1978.

POLITICAL BIOGRAPHY

CHERRY, GORDON E., 'The Place of Neville Chamberlain in British Town Planning', in (ed) *Shaping an Urban World: Planning in the Twentieth Century*, Mansell, London, 1980.

CROSSMAN, RICHARD, *The Diaries of a Cabinet Minister*, Vol. One, Hamish Hamilton and Jonathan Cape, London, 1975 (2 volumes).

DONOGHUE, BERNARD and JONES, G. W., *Herbert Morrison, Portrait of a Politician*, Weidenfeld and Nicolson, London, 1973.

FOOT, MICHAEL, *Aneurin Bevan*, Vol. I, 1897–1945, Macgibbon and Kee, London, 1962 (2 volumes).

JOHNSTON, THOMAS, *Memories*, Collins, London, 1952.

POLITICIANS AND PLANNING

CROSLAND, C. A. R., *The Future of Socialism*, Jonathan Cape, London, 1956.

LANSBURY, GEORGE, *My England*, Selwyn and Blount, London, 1934.

MACMILLAN, HAROLD, *The Middle Way*, Macmillan, London, 1938.

SIMON, E. D., *Rebuilding Britain – a Twenty Year Plan*, Victor Gollancz, London, 1945.

INDEX